Everything
the Bible Says
About
Angels
and
Demons

Everything
the Bible Says
About

Angels

and

Demons

BETHANY HOUSE PUBLISHERS

a division of Baker Publishing Group
Minneapolis, Minnesota

© 2012 by Bethany House Publishers

Compiled by Bob Newman
Series editor: Andy McGuire

Published by Bethany House Publishers
11400 Hampshire Avenue South
Bloomington, Minnesota 55438
www.bethanyhouse.com

Bethany House Publishers is a division of
Baker Publishing Group, Grand Rapids, Michigan

Printed in the United States of America

Library of Congress Cataloging-in-Publication Data
Everything the Bible says about angels and demons / [compiled by Robert O. Newman].
    p.   cm.
    Summary: "Included are all Bible passages about angels and demons arranged topically and with brief commentary"—Provided by publisher.
    Includes bibliographical references (p.   ) and index.
    ISBN 978-0-7642-0910-9 (pbk. : alk. paper)
    1. Angels—Biblical teaching. 2. Demonology—Biblical teaching. I. Newman, Robert O.
BS680.A48E96 2012
235—dc23   2011045023

In keeping with biblical principles of creation stewardship, Baker Publishing Group advocates the responsible use of our natural resources. As a member of the Green Press Initiative, our company uses recycled paper when possible. The text paper of this book is composed in part of post-consumer waste.

Contents

Introduction

Angels of Light and Angels of Darkness

When it comes to angels and demons, we believe. According to a 2007 Gallup poll, 75 percent of Americans affirm the existence of angels; almost as many (70 percent) believe the devil is real.

While much of that confidence stems from religious beliefs, popular culture also plays a role in advancing the idea that angels are watching over us—and that Satan and his demons are active in our world. Various media, however, often take creative liberties with the subject of spirits. Other faiths and cults add their own ideas about these beings. Public perceptions don't always match the reality described in the Bible.

What might it mean to "sleep like an angel"? Do angels rejoice when a bell sounds or when a lost soul repents? Do they look like chubby-cheeked flying babies or fairy princesses of Christmas décor? Actually, angels often have been mistaken for men; their appearance regularly has frightened those who've encountered them; they've fulfilled and delivered divine missions and messages as God's servants, as he's assigned them.

There's plenty we can discover in Scripture. Passages in *Everything the Bible Says About Angels and Demons* are presented in story or event context. Topical headings, summary comments, and background information make it quick and easy to learn what angels and demons are about.

The Old Testament

1

Angels and Demons
in the Pentateuch

The Pentateuch (or Torah) encompasses the Bible's first five books: Genesis, Exodus, Leviticus, Numbers, and Deuteronomy. In these we learn about the world's creation, its introduction to sin, and the early history of God's chosen people. From Eden through Israel's exodus from Egypt and journey in the wilderness, angels and demons appear in many memorable stories.

THE FALL OF HUMANKIND

Genesis 2 says Adam and Eve lived in a garden paradise filled with trees pleasing to the eye and good for food. They lived in a state of innocence, with no knowledge of good and evil, until a being later identified as Satan (see Revelation 12:9; 20:2) successfully tempted them to disobey God.

The serpent was more crafty than any of the wild animals the Lord God had made. He said to the woman, "Did God really say, 'You must not eat from any tree in the garden'?"

The woman said to the serpent, "We may eat fruit from the trees in the garden, but God did say, 'You must not eat fruit from the tree that is in the middle of the garden, and you must not touch it, or you will die.'"

"You will not certainly die," the serpent said to the woman. "For God knows that when you eat from it your eyes will be opened, and you will be like God, knowing good and evil."

When the woman saw that the fruit of the tree was good for food and pleasing to the eye, and also desirable for gaining wisdom, she took some and ate it. She also gave some to her husband, who was with her, and he ate it. Then the eyes of both of them were opened, and they realized they were naked; so they sewed fig leaves together and made coverings for themselves.

Then the man and his wife heard the sound of the Lord God as he was walking in the garden in the cool of the day, and they hid from the Lord God among the trees of the garden. But the Lord God called to the man, "Where are you?"

He answered, "I heard you in the garden, and I was afraid because I was naked; so I hid."

And he said, "Who told you that you were naked? Have you eaten from the tree that I commanded you not to eat from?"

The man said, "The woman you put here with me—she gave me some fruit from the tree, and I ate it."

Then the Lord God said to the woman, "What is this you have done?"

The woman said, "The serpent deceived me, and I ate" (GENESIS 3:1–13 NIV).

Satan tries to convince people that they can defy God and distort his words without suffering adverse consequences.

─────── **GOD SETS CHERUBIM TO GUARD EDEN** ───────

After Adam and Eve brought sin into the world by disobeying what God had told them, they were evicted from Eden, and God put angels known as cherubim on duty to ensure they couldn't return.

He drove out the man; and He placed cherubim at the east of the garden of Eden, and a flaming sword which turned every way, to guard the way to the tree of life. (GENESIS 3:24 NKJV)

Angels enforce God's laws and can act as guardians to protect sacred places. Satan seeks to separate people from God by enticing disobedience.

─────── **HAGAR AND ISHMAEL** ───────

After Abraham had received a vision that God would give him a son as an heir, his wife, Sarai, began to doubt that the Lord could use her to fulfill his promise. Impatiently, she urged Abraham to sleep with her maidservant, Hagar. Abraham did, and Hagar became pregnant. When the women began to resent each other, Sarai mistreated Hagar, who then fled the household.

The angel of the Lord found Hagar beside a spring of water in the desert, by the road to Shur. The angel said, "Hagar, Sarai's slave girl, where have you come from? Where are you going?"

Hagar answered, "I am running away from my mistress Sarai."

The angel of the Lord said to her, "Go home to your mistress and obey her." The angel also said, "I will give you so many descendants they cannot be counted."

The angel added,

"You are now pregnant,
        and you will have a son.
You will name him Ishmael,
        because the Lord has heard your cries.

Ishmael will be like a wild donkey.
He will be against everyone,
and everyone will be against him.
He will attack all his brothers.'"

The slave girl gave a name to the Lord who spoke to her: "You are 'God who sees me,'" because she said to herself, "Have I really seen God who sees me?" **(GENESIS 16:7–13 NCV)**.

The angel of the Lord has protected and delivered God's people and revealed God's plans for them. Scholarly opinions vary as to the identity of the Lord's angel. Because he speaks for God in the first person, often saying or promising what only God could say or do, many believe he isn't just an angelic messenger but a visible manifestation of God himself or of the pre-incarnate Messiah (Son of God, second person of the Trinity). Matthew Henry, for instance, said that the words "I will so increase your descendants" (KJV) show this angel to be "the eternal Word and Son of God." (Others suggest that, as God's personal messenger, this angel may have been given authority to speak on God's behalf and to be identified with the one who sent him.) Also see Genesis 21:17; 22:11–12, 15–18; 31:11–13; Exodus 3:1–6; 14:19; Numbers 22:21–35; 2 Samuel 24:16; 2 Kings 1:3; 1 Chronicles 21:16, 18; Zechariah 1:8–9.

SODOM AND GOMORRAH

In Genesis 18, Abraham pleads with God not to destroy Sodom for the sake of righteous people within its boundaries. The Lord agrees to spare the city if ten can be found, but evidently the ensuing head-count comes up short, because now two angels (who'd already visited Abraham) arrive to round up the righteous. They urge Abraham's nephew, Lot, to get his family out.

The two angels came to Sodom in the evening as Lot was sitting in the gate of Sodom. When Lot saw them, he rose to meet them and bowed down with his face to the ground.

And he said, "Now behold, my lords, please turn aside into your servant's house, and spend the night, and wash your feet; then you may rise early and go on your way." They said however, "No, but we shall spend the night in the square."

Yet he urged them strongly, so they turned aside to him and entered his house; and he prepared a feast for them, and baked unleavened bread, and they ate. **(GENESIS 19:1–3 NASB)**

Lot persuaded the men, actually angels (see Hebrews 13:2), to follow his suggestion. Angels inhabiting physical bodies may fuel them with food.

ANGELS PROTECT LOT

Men from the city had arrived to demand that Lot allow them to sexually assault his guests. Lot tried fervently to defend his home, yet as the mob was about to break down his door, the "men" inside came to the rescue.

The two angels reached out, pulled Lot into the house, and bolted the door. Then they blinded all the men, young and old, who were at the door of the house, so they gave up trying to get inside. **(GENESIS 19:10–11 NLT)**

Even in human form, angels have supernatural powers. They protected Lot and his family from harm even though they hadn't requested aid.

"Do you have any other relatives here in the city?" [the angels] asked. "Get them out of this place—your sons-in-law, sons, daughters, or anyone else. For we are about to destroy this city completely. The outcry against this place is so great it has reached the Lord, and he has sent us to destroy it."

So Lot rushed out to tell his daughters' fiancés, "Quick, get out of the city! The Lord is about to destroy it." But the young men thought he was only joking.

At dawn the next morning the angels became insistent. "Hurry," they said to Lot. "Take your wife and your two daughters who are here. Get out right now, or you will be swept away in the destruction of the city!"

When Lot still hesitated, the angels seized his hand and the hands of his wife and two daughters and rushed them to safety outside the city, for the Lord was merciful. When they were safely out of the city, one of the angels ordered, "Run for your lives! And don't look back or stop anywhere in the valley! Escape to the mountains, or you will be swept away!"

"Oh no, my lord!" Lot begged. "You have been so gracious to me and saved my life, and you have shown such great kindness. But I cannot go to the mountains. Disaster would catch up to me there, and I would soon die. See, there is a small village nearby. Please let me go there instead; don't you see how small it is? Then my life will be saved."

"All right," the angel said, "I will grant your request. I will not destroy the little village. But hurry! Escape to it, for I can do nothing until you arrive there."

Lot reached the village just as the sun was rising over the horizon. Then the Lord rained down fire and burning sulfur from the sky on Sodom and Gomorrah. He utterly destroyed them, along with the other cities and villages of the plain, wiping out all the people and every bit of vegetation. But Lot's wife looked back as she was following behind him, and she turned into a pillar of salt. (GENESIS 19:12–26 NLT)

God can send angels as agents of his wrath and in response to the pleas of his people. (Once again, too, they accepted Lot's request to adjust the plan.)

──────── HAGAR AND ISHMAEL ASKED TO LEAVE ────────

After Isaac was born, Sarah asked Abraham to get rid of Hagar and the son, Ishmael, whom Hagar had borne to Abraham. The next day, Abraham gave Hagar some food and water and sent them into the desert.

When the water was gone, she left the child under a shrub and went off, fifty yards or so. She said, "I can't watch my son die." As she sat, she broke into sobs.

Meanwhile, God heard the boy crying. The angel of God called from Heaven to Hagar, "What's wrong, Hagar? Don't be afraid. God has heard the boy and knows the fix he's in. Up now; go get the boy. Hold him tight. I'm going to make of him a great nation."

Just then God opened her eyes. She looked. She saw a well of water. She went to it and filled her canteen and gave the boy a long, cool drink.

God was on the boy's side as he grew up. He lived out in the desert and became a skilled archer. He lived in the Paran wilderness. And his mother got him a wife from Egypt. (**GENESIS 21:15–21 THE MESSAGE**)

Angels are sometimes heard but not seen. An angel's willingness or ability to help isn't necessarily dependent on a person's spiritual fitness. (Hagar had apparently forgotten God's promises, given up hope, and not thought to pray about the situation.) The "angel of God"/"angel of the Lord" may be the second person of the Trinity (see comments on Genesis 16:7–13).

──────────── THE NEAR-SACRIFICE OF ISAAC ────────────

God commanded Abraham, "Take your son, your only son, whom you love—Isaac—and go to the region of Moriah. Sacrifice him

ure as a burnt offering on a mountain I will show you" (22:1–2).
Proceeding as directed, Abraham was about to slay his son on the
altar when an angel intervened.

The angel of the Lord called out to him from heaven, "Abraham! Abraham!"

"Here I am," he replied.

"Do not lay a hand on the boy," he said. "Do not do anything to him. Now I know that you fear God, because you have not withheld from me your son, your only son." . . .

The angel of the Lord called to Abraham from heaven a second time and said, "I swear by myself, declares the Lord, that because you have done this and have not withheld your son, your only son, I will surely bless you and make your descendants as numerous as the stars in the sky and as the sand on the seashore. Your descendants will take possession of the cities of their enemies, and through your offspring all nations on earth will be blessed, because you have obeyed me" **(GENESIS 22:11–12, 15–18 NIV)**.

The angel of the Lord again speaks for God in the first person. See comments on Genesis 16:7–13 for more on "the angel of the Lord."

A Wife for Isaac

Abraham sends a servant to his homeland to find a wife for Isaac.

The Lord, the God of heaven, who brought me out of my father's household and my native land and who spoke to me and promised me on oath, saying, "To your offspring I will give this land"—he will send his angel before you so that you can get a wife for my son from there. **(GENESIS 24:7 NIV)**

God may summon angels to ensure the success of a person's mission.

18

JACOB'S LADDER

Jacob dreamed that there was a ladder resting on the earth and reaching up into heaven, and he saw angels of God going up and coming down the ladder. (GENESIS 28:12 NCV)

Angels are active spirits, observed John Wesley: "They ascend to give account of what they have done, and to receive orders; and descend to execute the orders they have received." In John 1:51, Jesus says he himself is the ladder by which there is interaction between heaven and earth.

JACOB'S DREAM ABOUT GOATS

I had a dream during the season when the flocks were mating. I saw that the only male goats who were mating were streaked, speckled, or spotted. The angel of God spoke to me in that dream and said, "Jacob!" I answered, "Yes!" The angel said, "Look! Only the streaked, speckled, or spotted male goats are mating. I have seen all the wrong things Laban has been doing to you. I am the God who appeared to you at Bethel, where you poured olive oil on the stone you set up on end and where you made a promise to me. Now I want you to leave here and go back to the land where you were born" (GENESIS 31:10–13 NCV).

Angels can be assigned to speak through dreams. Some suggest this "angel of God" (who says, "I am the God who appeared to you at Bethel") is the pre-incarnate Christ. See also comments on Genesis 16:7–13.

JACOB PREPARES TO MEET ESAU

Esau should have inherited what God promised to Abraham's descendants. But he thought so little of his inheritance that he traded

19

away his birthright to his younger brother for just a meal. After Jacob then impersonated Esau to cheat his brother out of their blind father's deathbed blessing, Esau vowed to kill him. Years later, Jacob was about to reencounter Esau.

As Jacob started on his way again, angels of God came to meet him. When Jacob saw them, he exclaimed, "This is God's camp!" **(GENESIS 32:1–2 NLT)**

Angels can assure people they're where God wants them to be and provide encouragement (which Jacob needed, for he'd soon learn that Esau was on his way with hundreds of men). God's people in distress should appeal to God, not angels. (As Matthew Henry noted, after encountering angels, Jacob did not seek their help but instead prayed to God [see vv. 9–12].)

JACOB WRESTLES WITH GOD

Jacob was left alone; and a Man wrestled with him until the breaking of day. Now when He saw that He did not prevail against him, He touched the socket of his hip; and the socket of Jacob's hip was out of joint as He wrestled with him. And He said, "Let Me go, for the day breaks."

But he said, "I will not let You go unless You bless me!"

So He said to him, "What is your name?"

He said, "Jacob."

And He said, "Your name shall no longer be called Jacob, but Israel; for you have struggled with God and with men, and have prevailed."

Then Jacob asked, saying, "Tell me Your name, I pray."

And He said, "Why is it that you ask about My name?" And He blessed him there.

So Jacob called the name of the place Peniel: "For I have seen God face to face, and my life is preserved" (GENESIS 32:24–30 NKJV).

Hosea 12:4 identifies this opponent of Jacob's as "the angel." Other verses (see Genesis 32:28, 30; Hosea 12:5) imply this "man" to be "the Lord's angel" (i.e., God's Son). See also comments on Genesis 16:7–13.

———————————— JACOB'S BLESSING ————————————

The Angel who has redeemed me from all evil, Bless the lads; Let my name be named upon them, and the name of my fathers Abraham and Isaac; and let them grow into a multitude in the midst of the earth. (GENESIS 48:16 NKJV)

Angels can save people out of harm from the evil around them.

———————————— MOSES AND THE BURNING BUSH ————————————

[Moses] came to Sinai, the mountain of God. There the angel of the Lord appeared to him in flames of fire coming out of a bush. Moses saw that the bush was on fire, but it was not burning up. So he said, "I will go closer to this strange thing. How can a bush continue burning without burning up?"

When the Lord saw Moses was coming to look at the bush, God called to him from the bush, "Moses, Moses!"

And Moses said, "Here I am."

Then God said, "Do not come any closer. Take off your sandals, because you are standing on holy ground. I am the God of your ancestors—the God of Abraham, the God of Isaac, and the God of Jacob." Moses covered his face because he was afraid to look at God. (EXODUS 3:1–6 NCV)

Some believe the Lord's angel appeared not inside the fire but as fire. He was recognized as an angel before witnesses realized God was speaking.

--------------- THE PARTING OF THE SEA ---------------

Israel's people had long endured oppression under the Egyptians, so God called upon Moses to lead them out of Egypt and into the Promised Land. After giving permission, Pharaoh changed his mind and pursued militarily.

The angel of God, who had been traveling in front of Israel's army, withdrew and went behind them. The pillar of cloud also moved from in front and stood behind them, coming between the armies of Egypt and Israel. Throughout the night the cloud brought darkness to the one side and light to the other side; so neither went near the other all night long. **(EXODUS 14:19–20 NIV)**

Angels can serve as agents of protection and deliverance, sometimes standing between God's people and physical harm. The pillar of cloud (not an angel) was a visible sign of God's presence.

--------- GOD'S ANGEL IS SENT TO PREPARE THE WAY ---------

In the Book of the Covenant (see Exodus 20:22–23:33), the Lord provides a speech for Moses to deliver to the Israelites, including the following:

I am sending an angel before you to protect you on your journey and lead you safely to the place I have prepared for you. Pay close attention to him, and obey his instructions. Do not rebel against him, for he is my representative, and he will not forgive your rebellion. But if you are careful to obey him, following all my instructions, then I will be an enemy to your enemies, and I will oppose those who oppose you. For my angel will go before you and bring you into the land of [your enemies]. **(EXODUS 23:20–23 NLT)**

Angels have personalities; they are not merely "forces" or "powers." They can offer guidance, instruction, and protection, and reveal information.

─────── CHERUBIM ON THE ARK OF THE COVENANT ───────

The Lord gave Moses instructions on constructing this ark (an ornate chest containing the two tablets of the Ten Commandments, a pot of manna, and Aaron's rod). The directions included the following details:

Make the Ark's cover—the place of atonement—from pure gold. It must be 45 inches long and 27 inches wide. Then make two cherubim from hammered gold, and place them on the two ends of the atonement cover. Mold the cherubim on each end of the atonement cover, making it all of one piece of gold. The cherubim will face each other and look down on the atonement cover. With their wings spread above it, they will protect it. . . . Put the atonement cover on top of the Ark. I will meet with you there and talk to you from above the atonement cover between the gold cherubim that hover over the Ark of the Covenant. **(EXODUS 25:17–22 NLT)**

By God's power, even the presence of cherubim figures gave protection.

── GOD'S ANGEL LEADS, DRIVES OUT ISRAEL'S ENEMIES ──

Go. Lead the people where I have told you, and my angel will lead you. **(EXODUS 32:34 NCV)**

Get going, you and the people you brought up from the land of Egypt. Go up to the land I swore to give to Abraham, Isaac, and Jacob. I told them, "I will give this land to your descendants." And I will send an angel before you to drive out [your enemies]. **(EXODUS 33:1–2 NLT)**

Angels can serve to deliver God's people to the place he has for them; they can remove obstacles and opposition.

SACRIFICES TO DEMONS FORBIDDEN

Moses speaks as the Lord commands. "They" are the children of Israel.

They shall no more offer their sacrifices to demons, after whom they have played the harlot. This shall be a statute forever for them throughout their generations. **(LEVITICUS 17:7 NKJV)**

God's people are never to worship or serve demons.

MOSES CREDITS AN ANGEL FOR DELIVERING ISRAEL

You know all the hardships we have been through. Our ancestors went down to Egypt, and we lived there a long time, and we and our ancestors were brutally mistreated by the Egyptians. But when we cried out to the Lord, he heard us and sent an angel who brought us out of Egypt. **(NUMBERS 20:14–16 NLT)**

God can send angels to deliver from trouble in response to cries for help.

BALAAM'S DONKEY AND THE LORD'S ANGEL

Moab's king, terrified by the Israelites' arrival, sent men to ask Balaam, a pagan prophet, to place a curse on Israel. He went with them to do so.

God's anger was aroused because he went, and the Angel of the Lord took His stand in the way as an adversary against him. And he was riding on his donkey, and his two servants were with him. Now the donkey saw the Angel of the Lord standing in the way with His drawn sword in His hand, and the donkey turned aside out of the way and went into the field. So Balaam struck the donkey to turn her back onto the road. Then the Angel of the Lord stood in a narrow path between the vineyards, with a wall on this side and a wall on that side. And when the donkey saw the Angel of the Lord, she pushed herself against the wall and crushed Balaam's foot against the wall; so he struck her again. Then the Angel of the Lord went further, and stood in a narrow place where there was no way to turn either to the right hand or to the left. And when the donkey saw the Angel of the Lord, she lay down under Balaam; so Balaam's anger was aroused, and he struck the donkey with his staff.

Then the Lord opened the mouth of the donkey, and she said to Balaam, "What have I done to you, that you have struck me these three times?"

And Balaam said to the donkey, "Because you have abused me. I wish there were a sword in my hand, for now I would kill you!"

So the donkey said to Balaam, "Am I not your donkey on which you have ridden, ever since I became yours, to this day? Was I ever disposed to do this to you?"

And he said, "No."

Then the Lord opened Balaam's eyes, and he saw the Angel of the Lord standing in the way with His drawn sword in His hand; and he bowed his head and fell flat on his face. And the Angel of the Lord said to him, "Why have you struck your donkey these three times? Behold, I have come out to stand against you, because your way is perverse before Me. The donkey saw Me and turned aside from Me these three times. If she had not turned aside from Me, surely I would also have killed you by now, and let her live."

And Balaam said to the Angel of the Lord, "I have sinned, for I did not know You stood in the way against me. Now therefore, if it displeases You, I will turn back."

The Angel of the Lord said to Balaam, "Go with the men, but only the word that I speak to you, that you shall speak" (**NUMBERS 22:22–35** NKJV).

This "angel" was prepared to deliver God's punishment (see also Genesis 16:7–13 on "the angel of the Lord"). Balaam bowed before the Lord's angel and was not admonished to worship only God; therefore, some maintain, this "angel" is the pre-incarnate Christ, worthy of such honor.

———————— SACRIFICES TO DEMONS CONDEMNED ————————

Near his life's end, Moses recites a song to the nation's leaders, recalling God's goodness to his people and the wickedness they exhibited in return.

They sacrificed unto devils, not to God; to gods whom they knew not, to new gods that came newly up, whom your fathers feared not. (**DEUTERONOMY 32:17** KJV)

People giving devotion to idols/false gods actually can be serving demons.

2
Angels and Demons
in the Books of History

⁓⁓⁓

The Old Testament's twelve historical books (Joshua, Judges, Ruth, 1 and 2 Samuel, 1 and 2 Kings, 1 and 2 Chronicles, Ezra, Nehemiah, and Esther) record nearly a thousand years of Israel's history. Beginning with the entrance into the Promised Land, they tell of the nation's rise, fall, captivity, and return from exile. As the story unfolds, we see angels (and also demons) at work.

— THE LORD'S ANGEL REBUKES ISRAEL'S DISOBEDIENCE —

The angel of the Lord went up from Gilgal to Bokim and said, "I brought you up out of Egypt and led you into the land that I swore to give to your ancestors. I said, 'I will never break my covenant with you, and you shall not make a covenant with the people of this land, but you shall break down their altars.' Yet you have disobeyed me. Why have you done this? And I have also said, 'I will not drive them out before you; they will become traps for you, and their gods will become snares to you'" (JUDGES 2:1–3 NIV).

Could "angel of the Lord" ever signify a different person? Angel means "messenger," so some suggest "angel of the Lord" could refer to a prophet or high priest—for instance, in Judges 6, an unnamed prophet delivers a similar message. Could the commute from Gilgal (not from the heavens) imply a human messenger? Many say no, this appearance (the angel again speaks for God in the first person) is consistent with others and likewise is a manifestation of God himself. (See comments for Genesis 16:7–13.)

──────── **THE ANGEL OF THE LORD PLACES A CURSE** ────────

"Let the people of Meroz be cursed," said the angel of the Lord.
    "Let them be utterly cursed,
because they did not come to help the Lord—
    to help the Lord against the mighty warriors."

(JUDGES 5:23 NLT)

As Israel battled the Canaanites, the people of Meroz offered no assistance. The Lord's angel punished them for refusing to help.

──────── **THE ANGEL OF THE LORD VISITS GIDEON** ────────

The angel of the Lord came and sat down under the oak tree at Ophrah. . . . Gideon . . . was separating some wheat from the chaff in a winepress to keep the wheat from the Midianites. The angel of the Lord appeared to Gideon and said, "The Lord is with you, mighty warrior!"

Then Gideon said, "Sir, if the Lord is with us, why are we having so much trouble? Where are the miracles our ancestors told us he did when the Lord brought them out of Egypt? But now he has left us and has handed us over to the Midianites."

The Lord turned to Gideon and said, "Go with your strength and save Israel from the Midianites. I am the one who is sending you."

But Gideon answered, "Lord, how can I save Israel? My family group is the weakest in Manasseh, and I am the least important member of my family."

The Lord answered him, "I will be with you. It will seem as if the Midianites you are fighting are only one man."

Then Gideon said to the Lord, "If you are pleased with me, give me proof that it is really you talking with me. Please wait here until I come back to you. Let me bring my offering and set it in front of you."

And the Lord said, "I will wait until you return."

So Gideon went in and cooked a young goat, and with twenty quarts of flour, made bread without yeast. Then he put the meat into a basket and the broth into a pot. He brought them out and gave them to the angel under the oak tree.

The angel of God said to Gideon, "Put the meat and the bread without yeast on that rock over there. Then pour the broth on them." And Gideon did as he was told. The angel of the Lord touched the meat and the bread with the end of the stick that was in his hand. Then fire jumped up from the rock and completely burned up the meat and the bread! And the angel of the Lord disappeared! Then Gideon understood . . . [and] cried out, "Lord God! I have seen the angel of the Lord face to face!"

But the Lord said to Gideon, "Calm down! Don't be afraid! You will not die!"

So Gideon built an altar there to worship the Lord and named it The Lord Is Peace. (JUDGES 6:11–24 NCV)

The Lord's angel may have appeared as an ordinary man (people could be slow to identify him). He inspired Gideon with courage and confidence, revealing what could be accomplished through God's presence and power.

THE BIRTH OF SAMSON

A man named Manoah from the tribe of Dan lived in the town of Zorah. His wife was unable to become pregnant, and they had no children. The angel of the Lord appeared to Manoah's wife and said, "Even though you have been unable to have children, you will soon become pregnant and give birth to a son. So be careful; you must not drink wine or any other alcoholic drink nor eat any forbidden food. You will become pregnant and give birth to a son, and his hair must never be cut. For he will be dedicated to God as a Nazirite from birth. He will begin to rescue Israel from the Philistines."

The woman ran and told her husband, "A man of God appeared to me! He looked like one of God's angels, terrifying to see. I didn't ask where he was from, and he didn't tell me his name. . . . "

Then Manoah prayed to the Lord, saying, "Lord, please let the man of God come back to us again and give us more instructions about this son who is to be born."

God answered Manoah's prayer, and the angel of God appeared once again to his wife as she was sitting in the field. But her husband, Manoah, was not with her. So she quickly ran and told her husband, "The man who appeared to me the other day is here again!"

Manoah ran back with his wife and asked, "Are you the man who spoke to my wife the other day?"

"Yes," he replied, "I am."

So Manoah asked him, "When your words come true, what kind of rules should govern the boy's life and work?"

The angel of the Lord replied, "Be sure your wife follows the instructions I gave her. She must not eat grapes or raisins, drink wine or any other alcoholic drink, or eat any forbidden food."

Then Manoah said to the angel of the Lord, "Please stay here until we can prepare a young goat for you to eat."

"I will stay," the angel of the Lord replied, "but I will not eat anything. However, you may prepare a burnt offering as a sacrifice to the Lord." (Manoah didn't realize it was the angel of the Lord.)

Then Manoah asked the angel of the Lord, "What is your name? For when all this comes true, we want to honor you."

"Why do you ask my name?" the angel of the Lord replied. "It is too wonderful for you to understand."

Then Manoah took a young goat and a grain offering and offered it on a rock as a sacrifice to the Lord. And as Manoah and his wife watched, the Lord did an amazing thing. As the flames from the altar shot up toward the sky, the angel of the Lord ascended in the fire. When Manoah and his wife saw this, they fell with their faces to the ground.

The angel did not appear again to Manoah and his wife. Manoah finally realized it was the angel of the Lord, and he said to his wife, "We will certainly die, for we have seen God!"

But his wife said, "If the Lord were going to kill us, he wouldn't have accepted our burnt offering and grain offering. He wouldn't have appeared to us and told us this wonderful thing and done these miracles."

When her son was born, she named him Samson. And the Lord blessed him as he grew up. (JUDGES 13:2–6, 8–24 NLT)

The Lord's angel—his name, even, is "too wonderful" to grasp— revealed specific instructions and plans. His physical appearance (in renderings of v. 6) is described as "very terrible," "awesome," "frightening."

——— KING SAUL TORMENTED BY AN EVIL SPIRIT ———

The Spirit of the Lord departed from Saul, and an evil spirit from the Lord terrorized him. Saul's servants then said to him, "Behold now, an evil spirit from God is terrorizing you. Let our lord now command your servants who are before you. Let them seek a man who is a skillful player on the harp; and it shall come about when the evil spirit from God is on you, that he shall play the harp with his hand, and you will be well." So Saul said to his servants, "Provide for me now a man who can play well and bring him to me." Then one of the young men said, "Behold, I have seen a son of Jesse the Bethlehemite who is a skillful musician, a mighty man of valor, a warrior, one prudent in speech, and a handsome man; and the Lord is with him." So Saul sent messengers to Jesse and said, "Send me your son David.". . . Whenever the evil spirit from God came to Saul, David would take the harp and play it with his hand; and Saul would be refreshed and be well, and the evil spirit would depart from him. . . .

[Again] an evil spirit from God came mightily upon Saul, and he raved in the midst of the house, while David was playing the harp with his hand, as usual; and a spear was in Saul's hand. Saul hurled the spear, for he thought, "I will pin David to the wall." But David escaped from his presence twice. . . .

[Again] there was an evil spirit from the Lord on Saul as he was sitting in his house with his spear in his hand, and David was playing the harp with his hand. Saul tried to pin David to the wall with the spear, but he slipped away out of Saul's presence, so that he stuck the spear into the wall. And David fled and escaped that night. **(1 SAMUEL 16:14–19, 23; 18:10–11; 19:9–10 NASB)**

Whether this involved demonic possession or mental illness, and whether the "spirit" was, God is not the author of evil—evil spirits are subject to him, and he permitted Saul's affliction. (Matthew Henry said that if God's Spirit departs from a man, sin and Satan will have possession by default.) An evil spirit can cause a tormented person to be a danger to others.

— DAVID (THRICE) COMPARED OR LIKENED TO AN ANGEL —

David fled to the Philistine city of Gath and served its king, Achish, who thought highly of him. Yet the military leaders questioned David's loyalty and persuaded the king he should not fight alongside them against Saul.

"But what have I done?" asked David. "What have you found against your servant from the day I came to you until now? Why can't I go and fight against the enemies of my lord the king?"

Achish answered, "I know that you have been as pleasing in my eyes as an angel of God; nevertheless, the Philistine commanders have said, 'He must not go up with us into battle'" **(1 SAMUEL 29:8–9 NIV).**

The commander of David's army, Joab, apparently became concerned about a dispute between David and Absalom, his son. So Joab sent for a "wise woman" from another town to appear before David, playing the part of a grieving widow, and told her what to say, including the following:

33

"May the words of my master the king give me rest. Like an angel of God, you know what is good and . . . bad. May the Lord your God be with you!". . .

The king said, "Did Joab tell you to say all these things?"

The woman answered, "As you live, my master the king, no one could avoid that question. You are right. Your servant Joab did tell me to say these things. Joab did it so you would see things differently. My master, you are wise like an angel of God who knows everything that happens on earth" (2 SAMUEL 14:17, 19–20 NCV).

Mephibosheth, Saul's surviving grandson, spoke to King David.

My master the king . . . my servant betrayed me. I told him to saddle my donkey so I could ride it and go with the king, for, as you know, I am lame. And then he lied to you about me. But my master the king has been like one of God's angels: he knew what was right and did it. Wasn't everyone in my father's house doomed? But you took me in and gave me a place at your table. What more could I ever expect or ask? (2 SAMUEL 19:26–28 THE MESSAGE)

> *(1) Achish's words were a compliment—he didn't believe in God, yet he saw in David attributes he'd associated with the angels he'd heard about. (2) People considered angels to possess profound wisdom and discernment. (3) Angels know what's true (reality) and right (God's will), and they do it.*

—— JUDGMENT ON DAVID'S SIN (2 SAMUEL 24:15-17) ——

See "The Lord's Angel Inflicts Punishment" (on 1 Chronicles 21:11-30).

DETAILS OF CHERUBIM FIGURES
IN SOLOMON'S TEMPLE

He made two cherubim, gigantic angel-like figures, from olive-wood. Each was fifteen feet tall. The outstretched wings of the cherubim (they were identical in size and shape) measured another fifteen feet. He placed the two cherubim, their wings spread, in the Inner Sanctuary. The combined wingspread stretched the width of the room, the wing of one cherub touched one wall, the wing of the other the other wall, and the wings touched in the middle. The cherubim were gold-plated. (1 KINGS 6:23–28 THE MESSAGE)

> *The figures were a visual reminder of banishment from Eden/separation from God because of sin (see Genesis 3:24). Cherubim were engraved elsewhere and woven into a curtain (see 1 Kings 6:29; 2 Chronicles 3:14).*

"OLD PROPHET" LIES ABOUT
RECEIVING ANGELIC MESSAGE

An "old prophet living in Bethel" learned that a "man of God" (i.e., a prophet) had arrived from Judah and was denouncing the altars and shrines to false gods. The Lord had forbidden the man to eat or drink at Bethel, but the "old prophet" persuades him to come to his home and eat.

[The "old prophet"] said, "I am also a prophet, just like you. And an angel came to me with a message from God: 'Bring him home with you, and give him a good meal!'" But the man was lying. So the holy man went home with him and they had a meal together. (1 KINGS 13:18–19 THE MESSAGE)

> *An angel's words carry authority but can be misrepresented or "invented."*

35

———————— THE LORD'S ANGEL FEEDS ELIJAH ————————

When she heard Elijah had killed Baal's prophets, Jezebel (Ahab's wife) sent a message pledging to kill him within a day. Terrified, he fled to Beersheba, then into the desert, where he prayed God would kill him.

[Elijah] lay down and slept under a juniper tree; and behold, there was an angel touching him, and he said to him, "Arise, eat." Then . . . there was at his head a bread cake baked on hot stones, and a jar of water. So he ate and drank and lay down again. The angel of the Lord came again a second time and touched him and said, "Arise, eat, because the journey is too great for you." So he arose and ate and drank, and went in the strength of that food forty days and forty nights to Horeb, the mountain of God. **(1 KINGS 19:5–8 NASB)**

The angel of the Lord (see comments for Genesis 16:7–13) met Elijah's physical needs with food that would sustain him for nearly six weeks.

——————THE LORD'S ANGEL GIVES A MESSAGE—————— ### TO ELIJAH FOR KING AHAZIAH

Ahaziah fell through the lattice in his upper chamber which was in Samaria, and became ill. So he sent messengers and said to them, "Go, inquire of Baal-zebub, the god of Ekron, whether I will recover from this sickness." But the angel of the Lord said to Elijah the Tishbite, "Arise, go up to meet the messengers of the king of Samaria and say to them, 'Is it because there is no God in Israel that you are going to inquire of Baal-zebub, the god of Ekron?' Now therefore thus says the Lord, 'You shall not come down from the bed where you have gone up, but you shall surely die'" **(2 KINGS 1:2–4 NASB)**.

The angel of the Lord acted as God's spokesman.

——— The Angel of the Lord Assures Elijah ———

Ahaziah twice sent a captain and fifty men to summon Elijah. Each time, fire from heaven consumed them. The third captain pleaded for his life.

The angel of the Lord said to Elijah, "Go down with [the captain]; do not be afraid of him." So he arose and went. **(2 KINGS 1:15 NKJV)**

The Lord's angel provided boldness to face the king and not give in to fear.

——— The Lord's Angel Kills 185,000 Assyrians (2 Kings 19:35) ———

See "An Angel Destroys the Assyrian Army" (on 2 Chronicles 32:21).

——— Satan Provokes David ———

Satan attempted to attack Israel by provoking David to count the Israelites. David said to Joab and the leaders of the people, "Go, count Israel from Beersheba to Dan. Bring me the results so that I may know how many people there are" **(1 CHRONICLES 21:1–2 GOD'S WORD)**.

God may use the devil to carry out his own purposes. Second Samuel 24 says God incited David to take the census; though Satan stands in opposition to God, ultimately he's under God's sovereign control.

——— The Lord's Angel Inflicts Punishment ———

After taking a census and then realizing he'd sinned in doing so, the prophet Gad informs David of the possible punishments from which he must choose. (Interpretations vary as to why his action was wrong.)

"This is what the Lord says: 'Take your choice: three years of famine, three months of being swept away before your enemies, with their swords overtaking you, or three days of the sword of the Lord—days of plague in the land, with the angel of the Lord ravaging every part of Israel.' Now then, decide how I should answer the one who sent me."

David said to Gad, "I am in deep distress. Let me fall into the hands of the Lord, for his mercy is very great; but do not let me fall into human hands."

So the Lord sent a plague on Israel, and seventy thousand men of Israel fell dead. And God sent an angel to destroy Jerusalem. But as the angel was doing so, the Lord saw it and relented concerning the disaster and said to the angel who was destroying the people, "Enough! Withdraw your hand." The angel of the Lord was then standing at the threshing floor of Araunah the Jebusite.

David looked up and saw the angel of the Lord standing between heaven and earth, with a drawn sword in his hand extended over Jerusalem. Then David and the elders, clothed in sackcloth, fell facedown.

David said to God, "Was it not I who ordered the fighting men to be counted? I, the shepherd, have sinned and done wrong. These are but sheep. What have they done? O Lord my God, let your hand fall upon me and my family, but do not let this plague remain on your people."

Then the angel of the Lord ordered Gad to tell David to go up and build an altar to the Lord on the threshing floor of Araunah the Jebusite. So David went up in obedience to the word that Gad had spoken in the name of the Lord.

While Araunah was threshing wheat, he turned and saw the angel; his four sons who were with him hid themselves. Then

David approached, and when Araunah looked and saw him, he left the threshing floor and bowed down before David with his face to the ground.

David said to him, "Let me have the site of your threshing floor so I can build an altar to the Lord, that the plague on the people may be stopped. Sell it to me at the full price.". . .

David built an altar to the Lord there and sacrificed burnt offerings and fellowship offerings. He called on the Lord, and the Lord answered him with fire from heaven on the altar of burnt offering.

Then the Lord spoke to the angel, and he put his sword back into its sheath. At that time, when David saw that the Lord had answered him on the threshing floor of Araunah the Jebusite, he offered sacrifices there. The tabernacle of the Lord, which Moses had made in the wilderness, and the altar of burnt offering were at that time on the high place at Gibeon. But David could not go before it to inquire of God, because he was afraid of the sword of the angel of the Lord. (1 CHRONICLES 21:11-22, 26-30 NIV)

The visible appearance of the Lord's angel, who sometimes spoke through prophets, was intended to reveal the plague as a punishment from God.

──────── AN ANGEL DESTROYS THE ASSYRIAN ARMY ────────

The Lord sent an angel who destroyed every mighty warrior, commander and officer in the camp of the king of Assyria. (2 CHRONICLES 32:21 NASB)

God may employ angels to exercise judgment on the enemies of his people.

3
Angels and Demons
in the Books of Poetry

❦

The books of poetry and wisdom are Job, Psalms, Proverbs, Ecclesiastes, and Song of Songs. The first two give information about angels and about Satan.

ANGELS ASSEMBLE BEFORE GOD; SATAN TWICE ACCUSES JOB

There was a day when the sons of God came to present themselves before the Lord, and Satan also came among them. The Lord said to Satan, "From where do you come?" Then Satan answered the Lord and said, "From roaming about on the earth and walking around on it." The Lord said to Satan, "Have you considered My servant Job? For there is no one like him on the earth, a blameless and upright man, fearing God and turning away from evil." Then Satan answered the Lord, "Does Job fear

God for nothing? Have You not made a hedge about him and his house and all that he has, on every side? You have blessed the work of his hands, and his possessions have increased in the land. But put forth Your hand now and touch all that he has; he will surely curse You to Your face." Then the Lord said to Satan, "Behold, all that he has is in your power, only do not put forth your hand on him." So Satan departed from the presence of the Lord. (JOB 1:6–12 NASB)

[Again] one day the members of the heavenly court came again to present themselves before the Lord, and the Accuser, Satan, came with them. "Where have you come from?" the Lord asked Satan.

Satan answered the Lord, "I have been patrolling the earth, watching everything that's going on."

Then the Lord asked Satan, "Have you noticed my servant Job? He is the finest man in all the earth. He is blameless—a man of complete integrity. He fears God and stays away from evil. And he has maintained his integrity, even though you urged me to harm him without cause."

Satan replied to the Lord, "Skin for skin! A man will give up everything he has to save his life. But reach out and take away his health, and he will surely curse you to your face!"

"All right, do with him as you please," the Lord said to Satan. "But spare his life." So Satan left the Lord's presence, and he struck Job with terrible boils from head to foot. (JOB 2:1–7 NLT)

These "sons of God" likely are angels. Many are surprised to find Satan (which means "adversary") in a heavenly meeting, yet clearly he's been allowed some access to God's presence. With permission, he has attacked believers by separating them from possessions or blessings in hopes of turning them from and even cursing God (see vv. 8–9), who allows these tests to strengthen faith. "Roaming about" may indicate Satan's observing the world and reporting on instances of people choosing sin instead of God.

Eliphaz Speaks of Angels' Fallibility and God's "Holy Ones"

Job's "friend" Eliphaz said he received a vision and heard a voice whose message included the following statements about angels and humans:

If God places no trust in his servants,
if he charges his angels with error,
how much more those who live in houses of clay,
whose foundations are in the dust? . . .
Call if you will, but who will answer you?
To which of the holy ones will you turn? **(JOB 4:18–19, 5:1 NIV)**

That this statement about angels isn't refuted elsewhere leads some to hold this vision as genuine and its insight truthful. (If that were correct, angels might err and not always have the Lord's full confidence.) Some say "holy ones" refers to God's angels and attests to their being set apart from sin. Others contend that "holy ones" may also (or instead) refer to the saints.

Elihu on an Angel as a Mediator

If there is an angel at their side
a messenger, one out of a thousand,
sent to tell them how to be upright,
and he is gracious to that person and says to God,
"Spare them from going down to the pit;
I have found a ransom for them—
let their flesh be renewed like a child's;

let them be restored as in the days of their youth" (JOB 33:23-25 NIV).

"Angel" may refer to a spirit being or a human messenger/prophet/ teacher.

GOD RESPONDS TO JOB

Where were you when I made the earth's foundation?
Tell me, if you understand.
Who marked off how big it should be? Surely you know!
Who stretched a ruler across it?
What were the earth's foundations set on,
or who put its cornerstone in place
while the morning stars sang together
and all the angels shouted with joy? (JOB 38:4-7 NCV).

The angels, created prior to the world's creation, rejoice at God's works.

DAVID CELEBRATES THE WONDER OF CREATION

What is man that You are mindful of him,
    And the son of man that You visit him?
For You have made him a little lower than the angels,
    And You have crowned him with glory and honor. (PSALM 8:4-5 NKJV)

Angels and people are distinct (we don't become angels when we die). In the created order, angels were slightly greater in dignity; once Adam and Eve chose sin, their status in God's kingdom fell. Hebrews 2:6-8 quotes this passage regarding Jesus, who, in humbling himself to become man, made it possible for Adam's descendants to regain their lost standing.

——— GOD RIDING CHERUBIM TO DAVID'S AID ———

In commemoration of victory, cherubim are depicted as God's "chariot."

He mounted the cherubim and flew;
he soared on the wings of the wind. **(PSALM 18:10 NIV)**

——— PRAISING THE LORD FOR DELIVERANCE ———

The angel of the Lord encampeth round about them that fear him, and delivereth them. **(PSALM 34:7 KJV)**

The Lord's angel protects those who fear God.

DAVID SEEKS GOD'S VENGEANCE AGAINST HIS OPPRESSORS

Let them be as chaff before the wind: and let the angel of the Lord chase them.

Let their way be dark and slippery: and let the angel of the Lord persecute them. **(PSALM 35:5–6 KJV)**

The Lord's angel was believed to pursue and punish his people's enemies.

——— REMEMBERING THE "FOOD OF ANGELS" ———

He rained down manna for them to eat;
he gave them bread from heaven.
They ate the food of angels!
God gave them all they could hold. **(PSALM 78:24–25 NLT)**

God provided despite his people's disobedience. Angels may or may not ever eat manna; perhaps they helped in its production or distribution. This also could have been a poetic way to describe food "from heaven."

<hr>

RECALLING GOD'S PLAGUES AGAINST EGYPT

He loosed on them his fierce anger—
    all his fury, rage, and hostility.
He dispatched against them
    a band of destroying angels. **(PSALM 78:49 NLT)**

While the KJV uses the term "evil angels," they themselves weren't evil; God used them to bring evil on Egypt. Matthew Henry said, "Good angels become evil angels to sinners. Those that make the holy God their enemy must never expect the holy angels to be their friends." (Others leave open the possibility that God used demons to carry out the plagues.)

<hr>

THE "SECRET PLACE" PSALM

The Lord is your protection;
    you have made God Most High your place of safety.
Nothing bad will happen to you;
    no disaster will come to your home.
He has put his angels in charge of you
    to watch over you wherever you go.
They will catch you in their hands
    so that you will not hit your foot on a rock.

(PSALM 91:9–12 NCV)

God may send angels to protect those who place their faith in him.

——————— A PSALM OF DAVID ———————

Bless the Lord, you His angels,
Mighty in strength, who perform His word,
Obeying the voice of His word!
Bless the Lord, all you His hosts,
You who serve Him, doing His will. **(PSALM 103:20–21 NASB)**

Angels are powerful; they obey God's voice, and they do his will.

——————— THE POWER OF NATURE AS "ANGELS" ———————

You make your angels winds
  and your servants flames of fire. **(PSALM 104:4 GOD'S WORD)**

God uses natural forces as if they were angels, for his purposes.

——————— ANGELS EXHORTED TO PRAISE GOD ———————

Praise him, all you angels.
  Praise him, all you armies of heaven. **(PSALM 148:2 NCV)**

4

Angels and Demons
in the Books of the Prophets

———⟐———

The Old Testament's last seventeen books feature prophets who spoke God's words revealed through dreams, visions, declarations, and divine appearances. These spokesmen called people to repentance, reminding them of past blessings and warning them of future judgment. They foretold Messiah's coming and promised a glorious future for those who obey God. Angels played prominent roles in the messages' transmission and interpretation.

——————— ISAIAH SEES SERAPHIM ———————

Through a vision, God called Isaiah to be a preacher and prophet.

It was in the year King Uzziah died that I saw the Lord. He was sitting on a lofty throne, and the train of his robe filled the

Temple. Attending him were mighty seraphim, each having six
wings. With two wings they covered their faces, with two they
covered their feet, and with two they flew. They were calling
out to each other,
"Holy, holy, holy is the Lord of Heaven's Armies!
The whole earth is filled with his glory!"
Their voices shook the Temple to its foundations, and the
entire building was filled with smoke.
Then I said, "It's all over! I am doomed, for I am a sinful man.
I have filthy lips, and I live among a people with filthy lips. Yet
I have seen the King, the Lord of Heaven's Armies."
Then one of the seraphim flew to me with a burning coal he
had taken from the altar with a pair of tongs. He touched my lips
with it and said, "See, this coal has touched your lips. Now your
guilt is removed, and your sins are forgiven" (ISAIAH 6:1–7 NLT).

*The Hebrew word for seraphim means "burning ones," which may
refer to appearance or passion for serving God (who used a seraph's
act to forgive Isaiah's sins). It may be that seraphim cover their faces
at God's throne as a shield from his glory and cover their feet in
reverence for holy ground.*

—— THE FALL OF SATAN AND/OR THE KING OF BABYLON ——

How you are fallen from heaven,
O Lucifer ["Day Star"], son of the morning!
How you are cut down to the ground,
You who weakened the nations!
For you have said in your heart:
"I will ascend into heaven,
I will exalt my throne above the stars of God;
I will also sit on the mount of the congregation
On the farthest sides of the north;

I will ascend above the heights of the clouds,
I will be like the Most High" **(ISAIAH 14:12–14 NKJV)**.

This passage appears in Isaiah's prophecy against Babylon. Many believe it refers to Satan's fall; others maintain it's about the defeat of Babylon's king only; others suggest Isaiah uses Satan's fall to illustrate Babylon's.

—— RECOUNTING THE LORD'S GOODNESS TO ISRAEL ——

In all their affliction he was afflicted, and the angel of his presence saved them: in his love and in his pity he redeemed them; and he bare them, and carried them all the days of old. **(ISAIAH 63:9 KJV)**

Angels showed God's mercy in deliverance. Some believe "angel of his presence" refers to the Trinity's second person, associated with promises of God's protection in the wilderness (Exodus 23:20; cf. Genesis 16:7–13).

———————— CHERUBIM IN EZEKIEL'S VISION ————————

When I looked, I saw a stormy wind coming from the north. There was a great cloud with a bright light around it and fire flashing out of it. Something that looked like glowing metal was in the center of the fire. Inside the cloud was what looked like four living creatures, who were shaped like humans, but each of them had four faces and four wings. Their legs were straight. Their feet were like a calf's hoofs and sparkled like polished bronze. The living creatures had human hands under their wings on their four sides. All four of them had faces and wings, and their wings touched each other. The living creatures did not turn when they moved, but each went straight ahead.

Their faces looked like this: Each living creature had a human face and the face of a lion on the right side and the face of an ox on the left side. And each one also had the face of an eagle. That was what their faces looked like. Their wings were spread out above. Each had two wings that touched one of the other living creatures and two wings that covered its body. Each went straight ahead. Wherever the spirit would go, the living creatures would also go, without turning. The living creatures looked like burning coals of fire or like torches. Fire went back and forth among the living creatures. It was bright, and lightning flashed from it. The living creatures ran back and forth like bolts of lightning.

Now as I looked at the living creatures, I saw a wheel on the ground by each of the living creatures with its four faces. The wheels and the way they were made were like this: They looked like sparkling chrysolite. All four of them looked the same, like one wheel crossways inside another wheel. When they moved, they went in any one of the four directions, without turning as they went. The rims of the wheels were high and frightening and were full of eyes all around.

When the living creatures moved, the wheels moved beside them. When the living creatures were lifted up from the ground, the wheels also were lifted up. Wherever the spirit would go, the living creatures would go. And the wheels were lifted up beside them, because the spirit of the living creatures was in the wheels. When the living creatures moved, the wheels moved. When the living creatures stopped, the wheels stopped. And when the living creatures were lifted from the ground, the wheels were lifted beside them, because the spirit of the living creatures was in the wheels.

Now, over the heads of the living creatures was something like a dome that sparkled like ice and was frightening. And under the dome the wings of the living creatures were stretched out straight toward one another. Each living creature also had two wings covering its body. I heard the sound of their wings, like the roaring sound of the sea, as they moved. It was like the voice of God Almighty, a roaring sound like a noisy army. When the living creatures stopped, they lowered their wings.

A voice came from above the dome over the heads of the living creatures. When the living creatures stopped, they lowered their wings. Now above the dome there was something that looked like a throne. It looked like a sapphire gem. And on the throne was a shape like a human. Then I noticed that from the waist up the shape looked like glowing metal with fire inside. From the waist down it looked like fire, and a bright light was all around. The surrounding glow looked like the rainbow in the clouds on a rainy day. It seemed to look like the glory of the Lord. So when I saw it, I bowed facedown on the ground and heard a voice speaking. (EZEKIEL 1:4-28 NCV)

The living creatures (identified as cherubim in Ezekiel 10:15) are winged, brightly glowing angels with humanlike hands but different feet. They stood upright; they could move like lightning; their faces may symbolize various attributes of God and his creation (e.g., strength, power, intelligence).

VISION OF GOD'S GLORY DEPARTING FROM THE TEMPLE

The Lord's glory dwelt in the wilderness tabernacle Moses had built; then, later, in Solomon's temple. But the people had defiled it with altars to other gods. God's protection left; Jerusalem became vulnerable to destruction.

I looked, and I saw the likeness of a throne of lapis lazuli above the vault that was over the heads of the cherubim. The Lord said to the man clothed in linen, "Go in among the wheels beneath the cherubim. Fill your hands with burning coals from among the cherubim and scatter them over the city." And as I watched, he went in.

Now the cherubim were standing on the south side of the temple when the man went in, and a cloud filled the inner court. Then the glory of the Lord rose from above the cherubim and moved to the threshold of the temple. The cloud filled the temple, and the court was full of the radiance of the glory of the Lord. The sound of the wings of the cherubim could be heard as far away as the outer court, like the voice of God Almighty when he speaks.

When the Lord commanded the man in linen, "Take fire from among the wheels, from among the cherubim," the man went in and stood beside a wheel. Then one of the cherubim reached out his hand to the fire that was among them. He took up some of it and put it into the hands of the man in linen, who took it and went out. (Under the wings of the cherubim could be seen what looked like human hands.)

I looked, and I saw beside the cherubim four wheels, one beside each of the cherubim; the wheels sparkled like topaz. As for their appearance, the four of them looked alike; each was like a wheel intersecting a wheel. As they moved, they would go in any one of the four directions the cherubim faced; the wheels did not turn about as the cherubim went. The cherubim went in whatever direction the head faced, without turning as they went. Their entire bodies, including their backs, their hands and their wings, were completely full of eyes, as were their four wheels. I heard the wheels being called "the whirling wheels." Each of the cherubim had four faces: One face was that of a cherub, the second the face of a human being, the third the face of a lion, and the fourth the face of an eagle.

Then the cherubim rose upward. These were the living creatures I had seen by the Kebar River. When the cherubim moved, the wheels beside them moved; and when the cherubim spread their wings to rise from the ground, the wheels did not leave their side. When the cherubim stood still, they also stood still; and when the cherubim rose, they rose with them, because the spirit of the living creatures was in them.

Then the glory of the Lord departed from over the threshold of the temple and stopped above the cherubim. While I watched, the cherubim spread their wings and rose from the ground, and as they went, the wheels went with them. They stopped at the entrance to the east gate of the Lord's house, and the glory of the God of Israel was above them.

These were the living creatures I had seen beneath the God of Israel by the Kebar River, and I realized that they were cherubim. Each had four faces and four wings, and under their wings was what looked like human hands. Their faces had the same appearance as those I had seen by the Kebar River. Each one went straight ahead. (EZEKIEL 10:1–22 NIV)

NEBUCHADNEZZAR'S GOLDEN IMAGE AND THE FIERY FURNACE

Babylon's king built a monument and ordered all to worship it on command or be burned alive. Three Israelites refused and said their God was able to save them. In the flames, the king saw a fourth man who looked like a "son of the gods" (v. 25). He called out the three; they emerged unharmed. He credited God for sending his angel to protect them.

Nebuchadnezzar said, "Praise the God of Shadrach, Meshach, and Abednego. He sent his angel and saved his servants, who trusted him. They disobeyed the king and risked their lives so that they would not have to honor or worship any god except their own God" (DANIEL 3:28 GOD'S WORD).

────────── DANIEL IN THE LIONS' DEN ──────────

Darius, the Persian king, decreed that anyone who prayed to anyone but him would be thrown to the lions. Envious administrators accused Daniel.

"Daniel, who is one of the exiles from Judah, pays no attention to you, Your Majesty, or to the decree you put in writing. He still prays three times a day." When the king heard this, he was greatly distressed; he was determined to rescue Daniel and made every effort until sundown to save him.

Then the men went as a group to King Darius and said to him, "Remember, Your Majesty, that according to the law of the Medes and Persians no decree or edict that the king issues can be changed."

So the king gave the order, and they brought Daniel and threw him into the lions' den. The king said to Daniel, "May your God, whom you serve continually, rescue you!"

A stone was brought and placed over the mouth of the den, and the king sealed it with his own signet ring and with the rings of his nobles, so that Daniel's situation might not be changed. Then the king returned to his palace and spent the night without eating and without any entertainment being brought to him. And he could not sleep.

At the first light of dawn, the king got up and hurried to the lions' den. When he came near the den, he called to Daniel in an anguished voice, "Daniel, servant of the living God, has your God, whom you serve continually, been able to rescue you from the lions?"

Daniel answered, "May the king live forever! My God sent his angel, and he shut the mouths of the lions. They have not hurt me, because I was found innocent in his sight. Nor have I ever done any wrong before you, Your Majesty" (DANIEL 6:13–22 NIV).

──────── GABRIEL SENT TO INTERPRET AND FORETELL ────────

While I, Daniel, was trying to make sense of what I was seeing, suddenly there was a humanlike figure standing before me.

Then I heard a man's voice from over by the Ulai Canal calling out, "Gabriel, tell this man what is going on. Explain the vision to him." He came up to me, but when he got close I became terrified and fell facedown on the ground.

He said, "Understand that this vision has to do with the time of the end." As soon as he spoke, I fainted, my face in the dirt. But he picked me up and put me on my feet.

And then he continued, "I want to tell you what is going to happen as the judgment days of wrath wind down, for there is going to be an end to all this" (DANIEL 8:15–19 THE MESSAGE).

I went on praying and confessing my sin and the sin of my people, pleading with the Lord my God for Jerusalem, his holy mountain. As I was praying, Gabriel, whom I had seen in the earlier vision, came swiftly to me at the time of the evening sacrifice. He explained to me, "Daniel, I have come here to give you insight and understanding. The moment you began praying, a command was given. And now I am here to tell you what it was, for you are very precious to God. Listen carefully so that you can understand the meaning of your vision" (DANIEL 9:20–23 NLT).

Daniel was terrified even though Gabriel appeared "humanlike."
Angels can respond to prayer so quickly as to bring an answer as

the request is being made. They can provide understanding and convey God's great love.

THE ARCHANGEL MICHAEL; DANIEL'S VISION OF "A MAN"

On the twenty-fourth day of the first month, I was standing beside the great Tigris River. While standing there, I looked up and saw a man dressed in linen clothes with a belt of fine gold wrapped around his waist. His body was like shiny yellow quartz. His face was bright like lightning, and his eyes were like fire. His arms and legs were shiny like polished bronze, and his voice sounded like the roar of a crowd.

I, Daniel, was the only person who saw the vision. The men with me did not see it, because they were so frightened that they ran away and hid. So I was left alone. . . . I lost my strength, my face turned white like a dead person, and I was helpless. Then I heard the man in the vision speaking. As I listened, I fell into a deep sleep with my face on the ground.

Then a hand touched me and set me on my hands and knees. I was so afraid that I was shaking. The man in the vision said to me, "Daniel, God loves you very much. Think carefully about the words I will speak to you, and stand up, because I have been sent to you." When he said this, I stood up, but I was still shaking.

Then the man said to me, "Daniel, do not be afraid. Some time ago you decided to get understanding and to humble yourself before your God. Since that time God has listened to you, and I have come because of your prayers. But the prince of Persia has been fighting against me for twenty-one days. Then Michael, one of the most important angels, came to help me, because I had been left there with the king of Persia. Now I have come to explain to you what will happen to your people, because the vision is about a time in the future."

While he was speaking to me, I bowed facedown and could not speak. Then one who looked like a man touched my lips, so I opened my mouth and started to speak. I said to the one standing in front of me, "Master, I am upset and afraid because of what I saw in the vision. I feel helpless. Master, how can I, your servant, talk with you? My strength is gone, and it is hard for me to breathe."

The one who looked like a man touched me again and gave me strength. He said, "Daniel, don't be afraid. God loves you very much. Peace be with you. Be strong now; be courageous."

When he spoke to me, I became stronger and said, "Master, speak, since you have given me strength."

Then he said, "Daniel, do you know why I have come to you? Soon I must go back to fight against the prince of Persia. When I go, the prince of Greece will come, but I must first tell you what is written in the Book of Truth. No one stands with me against these enemies except Michael, the angel ruling over your people.

In the first year that Darius the Mede was king, I stood up to support Michael in his fight against the prince of Persia. (DANIEL 10:4–11:1 NCV)

> *The "man" in white linen may have been an angel or the second person of the Trinity (see Revelation 1:12–16). It's commonly held that in fighting the prince of Persia, the archangel Michael and the "man" in white were engaged in spiritual warfare with Satan or one of his demons.*

——— RESURRECTION IN THE GREAT TRIBULATION ———

> *The "man" in white (see Daniel 10) gives revelation about the end times.*

That's when Michael, the great angel-prince, champion of your people, will step in. It will be a time of trouble, the worst trouble the world has ever seen. But your people will be saved from the trouble, every last one found written in the Book. Many who have been long dead and buried will wake up, some to eternal life, others to eternal shame.

Men and women who have lived wisely and well will shine brilliantly, like the cloudless, star-strewn night skies. And those who put others on the right path to life will glow like stars forever. **(DANIEL 12:1–3 THE MESSAGE)**

The archangel Michael fights on Israel's behalf (some suggest he is Israel's guardian angel) and will come to her aid during the great tribulation.

——— HOSEA RECALLS JACOB'S STRUGGLE ———

When Jacob wrestled with the angel and won,
    he cried and asked for his blessing.
Later, God met with him at Bethel
    and spoke with him there.
(HOSEA 12:4 NCV; *see* **GENESIS 32:24–30)**

——— ZECHARIAH'S VISION (HORSES AND HORNS) ———

[Zechariah] asked the angel . . . "My lord, what do these horses mean?"

"I will show you," the angel replied.

The rider standing among the myrtle trees then explained, "They are the ones the Lord has sent out to patrol the earth."

Then the other riders reported to the angel of the Lord, who was standing among the myrtle trees, "We have been patrolling the earth, and the whole earth is at peace."

Upon hearing this, the angel of the Lord prayed this prayer: "O Lord of Heaven's Armies, for seventy years now you have been angry with Jerusalem and the towns of Judah. How long until you again show mercy to them?" And the Lord spoke kind and comforting words to the angel who talked with me.

Then the angel said to me, "Shout this message for all to hear: 'This is what the Lord of Heaven's Armies says: My love for Jerusalem and Mount Zion is passionate and strong. But I am very angry with the other nations that are now enjoying peace and security. I was only a little angry with my people, but the nations inflicted harm on them far beyond my intentions. . . .'"

Then I looked up and saw four animal horns. "What are these?" I asked the angel who was talking with me.

He replied, "These horns represent the nations that scattered Judah, Israel, and Jerusalem" (ZECHARIAH 1:9–15, 18–19 NLT).

The interpreting angel acted as messenger between Zechariah and the Lord's angel, who here intercedes with the Lord of Heaven's Armies (God the Father) on his people's behalf. (See comments on Genesis 16:7–13.)

ZECHARIAH'S VISION OF A "YOUNG MAN" MEASURING JERUSALEM

While the angel who was speaking to me was leaving, another angel came to meet him and said to him: "Run, tell that young man, 'Jerusalem will be a city without walls because of the great number of people and animals in it. And I myself will be a wall of fire around it,' declares the Lord, 'and I will be its glory within'" (ZECHARIAH 2:3–5 NIV).

Some say this "young man" is the Lord's angel (believed to be Christ); others say he's another angel, or a representation of Nehemiah.

──────── ZECHARIAH'S VISION OF THE HIGH PRIEST ────────

The angel showed me Jeshua the high priest standing before the angel of the Lord. The Accuser, Satan, was there at the angel's right hand, making accusations against Jeshua. And the Lord said to Satan, "I, the Lord, reject your accusations, Satan. Yes, the Lord, who has chosen Jerusalem, rebukes you. This man is like a burning stick that has been snatched from the fire."

Jeshua's clothing was filthy as he stood there before the angel. So the angel said to the others standing there, "Take off his filthy clothes." And turning to Jeshua he said, "See, I have taken away your sins, and now I am giving you these fine new clothes."

Then I said, "They should also place a clean turban on his head." So they put a clean priestly turban on his head and dressed him in new clothes while the angel of the Lord stood by.

Then the angel of the Lord spoke very solemnly to Jeshua and said, "This is what the Lord of Heaven's Armies says: If you follow my ways and carefully serve me, then you will be given authority over my Temple and its courtyards. I will let you walk among these others standing here" (ZECHARIAH 3:1-7 NLT).

The Lord's angel has authority to cleanse people of sin. Assuming he is the second person of the Trinity, God the Son here speaks on God the Father's behalf. (See also comments on Genesis 16:7-13 and Job 1:6-12; 2:1-7.)

ZECHARIAH'S VISION OF A GOLD LAMP STAND AND OLIVE TREES

The angel who was speaking with me returned and woke me up as one might wake up someone who is sleeping. He asked me, "What do you see?"

I answered, "I see a solid gold lamp stand with a bowl on top and seven lamps on it. There are seven spouts for each lamp that is on top of it. There are also two olive trees beside it, one on the right of the bowl and the other on its left.". . . "What do these things mean, sir?"

Then the angel asked me, "Don't you know what they mean?"

"No, sir," I answered.

Then he replied, "This is the word the Lord spoke to Zerubbabel: You won't succeed by might or by power, but by my Spirit, says the Lord of Armies. What a high mountain you are! In front of Zerubbabel you will become a plain. He will bring out the topmost stone with shouts of 'Blessings, blessings on it!'". . .

I asked the angel, "What do these two olive trees at the right and the left of the lamp stand mean? . . . What is the meaning of the two branches from the olive trees next to the two golden pipes that are pouring out gold?"

He asked me, "Don't you know what these things mean?"

"No, sir," I answered.

So he said, "These are the two anointed ones who are standing beside the Lord of the whole earth" (ZECHARIAH 4:1–7, 11–14 GOD'S WORD).

The angel initiates conversation about what he sees to reveal the vision's meaning. He establishes its authenticity as a divine revelation by having Zechariah admit that he doesn't know what the vision's objects mean.

—— ZECHARIAH'S VISION OF A WOMAN IN A BASKET ——

The angel . . . said to me, "Look up and see what is appearing."

I asked, "What is it?"

He replied, "It is a basket." And he added, "This is the iniquity of the people throughout the land."

Then the cover of lead was raised, and there in the basket sat a woman! He said, "This is wickedness," and he pushed her back into the basket and pushed the lead cover down on it.

Then I looked up—and there before me were two women, with the wind in their wings! They had wings like those of a stork, and they lifted up the basket between heaven and earth.

"Where are they taking the basket?" I asked. . . .

"To the country of Babylonia to build a house for it. When the house is ready, the basket will be set there in its place" (ZECHARIAH 5:5-11 NIV).

The angel draws focus to what he wants observed/questioned. The winged women may be female-looking angels; some, noting that the stork was seen as unclean, say they represented ungodly nations (Assyria and Babylon).

─────── ZECHARIAH'S VISION OF FOUR CHARIOTS ───────

Zechariah saw four chariots coming out from between two mountains, each pulled by a different colored horse.

[I asked,] "What are these, my lord?" The angel replied to me, "These are the four spirits of heaven, going forth after standing before the Lord of all the earth, with one of which the black horses are going forth to the north country; and the white ones go forth after them, while the dappled ones go forth to the south country. When the strong ones went out, they were eager to go to patrol the earth." And He said, "Go, patrol the earth." So they patrolled the earth. Then He cried out to me . . . "See, those who are going to the land of the north have appeased My wrath in the land of the north" (ZECHARIAH 6:4-8 NASB).

The spirits who go forth likely are angels acting as agents of God's wrath.

——————— GOD'S PROTECTION OVER ISRAEL ———————

In that day the Lord will defend the inhabitants of Jerusalem; the one who is feeble among them . . . shall be like David, and the house of David shall be like God, like the Angel of the Lord before them. **(ZECHARIAH 12:8 NKJV)**

In the end, when Jerusalem is attacked, God's protection will be like what Israel had when his angel led them out of Egypt into the Promised Land.

Section Two

The New Testament

5
Angels and Demons
and Jesus

The books of Matthew, Mark, Luke, and John (the Gospels) give eyewitness accounts of Jesus Christ's life and ministry on earth, including encounters with angels and demons. The *Gospel* (which means "good news") is that Jesus' death and resurrection have made salvation from sin possible.

Certain events and teachings are recorded by more than one book; some pertinent duplicate accounts are omitted. References for some companion passages are included within this chapter.

As to in-person biblical appearances, many believe Jesus is the Old Testament's "angel of the Lord." He also appears in Acts and the Revelation.

────────── THE BIRTH OF JESUS CHRIST ──────────

Joseph learned that Mary, his virgin fiancée, was pregnant. Not wanting to disgrace her publicly, he was thinking he'd quietly break the engagement.

An angel of the Lord appeared to him in a dream. "Joseph, son of David," the angel said, "do not be afraid to take Mary as your wife. For the child within her was conceived by the Holy Spirit. And she will have a son, and you are to name him Jesus, for he will save his people from their sins."

All of this occurred to fulfill the Lord's message through his prophet:

"Look! The virgin will conceive a child!
She will give birth to a son,
and they will call him Immanuel,
which means 'God is with us.'"

When Joseph woke up, he did as the angel of the Lord commanded and took Mary as his wife. **(MATTHEW 1:20–24 NLT)**

This may have been the angel (Gabriel) who appeared to Zechariah and to Mary (see Luke 1) in actual visits rather than through a dream. "An" angel of the Lord, this isn't "the" angel of the Lord, who many believe to have been God's Son (see comments on Genesis 16:7–13).

ESCAPE TO EGYPT

"Magi" sought the one born "King of the Jews." In Jerusalem, Herod directed them while instructing them to return with information. They found Jesus and worshiped him but were warned in a dream not to go back to Herod, who then ordered all children under two in Bethlehem to be killed.

An angel of the Lord appeared to Joseph in a dream. "Get up! Flee to Egypt with the child and his mother. . . . Stay there until I tell you to return, because Herod is going to search for the child to kill him" **(MATTHEW 2:13 NLT)**.

Angels protected Jesus from harm. By not calling Jesus "Joseph's son," the angel confirms what few knew—God's Spirit had conceived the child.

———————————— RETURN FROM EGYPT ————————————

After Herod was dead, an angel of the Lord appeared in a dream to Joseph in Egypt. The angel said to him, "Get up, take the child and his mother, and go to Israel. Those who tried to kill the child are dead." Joseph got up, took the child and his mother, and went to Israel. (MATTHEW 2:19-21 GOD'S WORD)

———————————— SATAN'S TEMPTATION OF JESUS ————————————

Jesus was led up by the Spirit into the wilderness to be tempted by the devil. And when He had fasted forty days and forty nights, afterward He was hungry. Now when the tempter came to Him, he said, "If You are the Son of God, command that these stones become bread."

But He answered and said, "It is written, 'Man shall not live by bread alone, but by every word that proceeds from the mouth of God.'"

Then the devil took Him up into the holy city, set Him on the pinnacle of the temple, and said to Him, "If You are the Son of God, throw Yourself down. For it is written: 'He shall give His angels charge over you,' and, 'In their hands they shall bear you up, lest you dash your foot against a stone.'"

Jesus said to him, "It is written again, 'You shall not tempt the Lord your God.'"

Again, the devil took Him up on an exceedingly high mountain, and showed Him all the kingdoms of the world and their glory. And he said to Him, "All these things I will give You if You will fall down and worship me."

Then Jesus said to him, "Away with you, Satan! For it is written, 'You shall worship the Lord your God, and Him only you shall serve.'"

Then the devil left Him, and behold, angels came and ministered to Him. (MATTHEW 4:1–11 NKJV; *also see* MARK 1:12–13; LUKE 4:2–13)

Angels nourished Jesus with food and fellowship. While Adam failed when tempted, infecting our race with sin, Jesus overcame Satan's lies with truth and proved himself worthy of being the Savior from sin. "The devil" (or "slanderer") knows God's Word too and seeks to distort it. He knew that Jesus is God's Son; he tried to get Jesus to take his bait by appealing to his humanity. Some believe Satan could have offered the kingdoms to Jesus as a real temptation only if he really controlled them; others contend the "god of this world" (see 2 Corinthians 4:4) merely exerts limited influence.

ON DOING GOD'S WILL

Not everyone who says to Me, "Lord, Lord," shall enter the kingdom of heaven, but he who does the will of My Father in heaven [will enter]. Many will say to Me in that day, "Lord, Lord, have we not prophesied in Your name, cast out demons in Your name, and done many wonders in Your name?" And then I will declare to them, "I never knew you; depart from Me, you who practice lawlessness!" (MATTHEW 7:21–23 NKJV).

We can't earn salvation. Anything on the outside is worthless that doesn't match who we are inside. God knows our hearts; if they aren't his, even seemingly "impressive" acts—like exorcism—are of no value to us.

─────── CASTING OUT DEMONS, HEALING THE SICK ───────

In the evening the people brought him many who were possessed by demons. He forced the evil spirits out of people with a command and cured everyone who was sick. (MATTHEW 8:16 GOD'S WORD)

Demons obeyed Jesus, who constantly demonstrated his power over Satan.

─────── HEALING A MAN WHO COULDN'T SPEAK ───────

A man who was demon-possessed and could not talk was brought to Jesus. And when the demon was driven out, the man who had been mute spoke. The crowd was amazed and said, "Nothing like this has ever been seen in Israel" (MATTHEW 9:32–33 NIV).

Demons can hinder speech. "Christ's cures strike at the root, and remove the effect by taking away the cause; they open the lips, by breaking Satan's power in the soul" (Matthew Henry).

─────── SENDING OUT THE TWELVE ───────

Jesus called his twelve disciples to him and gave them authority to drive out impure spirits and to heal every disease and sickness. . . . "Heal the sick, raise the dead, cleanse those who have leprosy, drive out demons. Freely you have received, freely give" (MATTHEW 10:1, 8 NIV; *also see* MARK 3:13–15).

They received ability (power) and permission (authority) to expel demons.

────── **EXPLAINING THE PARABLE OF THE WEEDS** ──────

The enemy who planted the weeds among the wheat is the devil. The harvest is the end of the world, and the harvesters are the angels.

Just as the weeds are sorted out and burned in the fire, so it will be at the end of the world. The Son of Man will send his angels, and they will remove from his Kingdom everything that causes sin and all who do evil. **(MATTHEW 13:39–41 NLT)**

Perhaps Satan scatters hypocrites/heretics among true followers. Or, "weeds" may refer not to unbelievers in the professing church but to all who belong to Satan as a result of not being Christ's. At the world's end, angels will separate believers from unbelievers.

────────── **THE PARABLE OF THE NET** ──────────

The kingdom of heaven is like a net that was thrown into the sea. It gathered all kinds of fish. When it was full, they pulled it to the shore. Then they sat down, gathered the good fish into containers, and threw the bad ones away. The same thing will happen at the end of time. The angels will go out and separate the evil people from people who have God's approval. Then the angels will throw the evil people into a blazing furnace. **(MATTHEW 13:47–50 GOD'S WORD)**

Angels will participate in the judgment of humankind.

────────── **THE SON OF MAN'S RETURN** ──────────

The Son of Man will come with his angels in his Father's glory. Then he will pay back each person based on what that person has done. **(MATTHEW 16:27 GOD'S WORD;** *also see* **MARK 8:38)**

Angels will accompany Jesus at his second coming.

―――――――― "CHILDREN'S ANGELS" ――――――――

See that you do not despise one of these little ones, for I say to you that their angels in heaven continually see the face of My Father who is in heaven. (MATTHEW 18:10 NASB)

That these angels see God's face attests to their holiness. This verse often is cited in support of guardian angels. Some say these aren't only for children but for all God's people. Others say that while angels keep watch, there's no indication that protective care is limited to one guardian angel.

――――― RESURRECTION, MARRIAGE, AND HEAVEN ―――――

When people rise from the dead, they will not marry, nor will they be given to someone to marry. They will be like the angels in heaven. (MATTHEW 22:30 NCV; *also see* MARK 12:25; LUKE 20:34–36)

Angels don't procreate or live in family units. Luke 20:34–36 (NLT) adds, "Marriage is for people here on earth. But in the age to come, those worthy of being raised from the dead . . . will never die again. In this respect they will be like angels . . . children of God and children of the resurrection."

―――――― THE SON OF MAN'S REAPPEARANCE ――――――

He will use a loud trumpet to send his angels all around the earth, and they will gather his chosen people from every part of the world. (MATTHEW 24:31 NCV; *also see* MARK 13:27)

Angels will gather all those saved by grace upon placing faith in God.

—————— THE JUDGMENT: THE SHEEP AND THE GOATS ——————

When the Son of man shall come in his glory, and all the holy angels with him, then shall he sit upon the throne of his glory. . . .

[He will say to the unbelievers,] "Depart from me, ye cursed, into everlasting fire, prepared for the devil and his angels" (MATTHEW 25:31, 41 KJV).

Not all translations include "holy," and some speculate that evil angels (demons) likewise will be on hand to prey on those who aren't Christ's true followers. Horrific, never-ending punishment awaits Satan and his demons.

—————————— THE ARREST OF JESUS ——————————

Judas arrived to hand over Jesus to armed men sent by the religious leaders. As they stepped forward, a defender drew his sword and cut off the ear of the high priest's servant; Jesus reprimanded him.

Do you think I cannot call on my Father, and he will at once put at my disposal more than twelve legions of angels? (MATTHEW 26:53 NIV)

A Roman legion consisted of about six thousand soldiers. In a literal sense, more than seventy-two thousand angels were available to aid Jesus.

————————— THE RESURRECTION OF JESUS —————————

After the Sabbath, as the first day of the week began to dawn, Mary Magdalene and the other Mary came to see the tomb. And behold, there was a great earthquake; for an angel of the Lord descended from heaven, and came and rolled back the stone from the door, and sat on it. His countenance was like lightning, and his clothing as white as snow. And the guards shook for fear of him, and became like dead men.

But the angel answered and said to the women, "Do not be afraid, for I know that you seek Jesus who was crucified. He is not here; for He is risen, as He said. Come, see the place where the Lord lay. And go quickly and tell His disciples that He is risen from the dead, and indeed He is going before you into Galilee; there you will see Him. Behold, I have told you" (MATTHEW 28:1–7 NKJV; *also see* MARK 16:1–8; LUKE 24:1–8; JOHN 20:11–13).

An angel moved the stone to show the tomb already was empty. The angels appeared in human form, though in "gleaming" or "dazzling" garments, and asked, "Why do you seek the living among the dead?" (Luke 24:4–5). They indicated that the women should be expecting the risen Savior, as Jesus had told his followers about his imminent death and resurrection.

Silencing Demons

After the sun was down, they brought sick and evil-afflicted people to him, the whole city lined up at his door! He cured their sick bodies and tormented spirits. Because the demons knew his true identity, he didn't let them say a word. (MARK 1:32–34 THE MESSAGE; *also see* LUKE 4:41)

Demons knew that Jesus is God's Son. He may have prohibited them to speak of this because the time hadn't arrived for him to be revealed as Messiah and/or it's inappropriate for demons to proclaim the gospel.

Jesus and Beelzebub

The teachers of the law who came down from Jerusalem said, "He is possessed by Beelzebub! By the prince of demons he is driving out demons."

. . . [Jesus spoke] to them in parables: "How can Satan drive out Satan? If a kingdom is divided against itself, that kingdom cannot stand. If a house is divided against itself, that house cannot stand. And if Satan opposes himself and is divided, he cannot stand; his end has come" (MARK 3:22–26 NIV).

"Beelzebub" is based on a Hebrew word meaning "lord of the flies." Satan using Jesus to immobilize Satan's workers is absurd. The leaders tried to join them because the exorcisms' supernatural nature was undeniable.

THE PARABLE OF THE SOWER

The farmer is like a person who plants God's message in people. Sometimes the teaching falls on the road. This is like the people who hear the teaching of God, but Satan quickly comes and takes away the teaching that was planted in them. (MARK 4:14–15 NCV; *also see* MATTHEW 13:1–23; LUKE 8:4–15)

Some suggest Satan is able to snatch away the truth "on the surface" if the listener's heart is hard. Others contend Satan tries to distract the listener's mind with other thoughts before God's message sinks in or takes root.

HEALING A DEMON-POSSESSED MAN

A man possessed by an evil spirit came out from a cemetery to meet [Jesus]. This man lived among the burial caves and could no longer be restrained, even with a chain. Whenever he was put into chains and shackles—as he often was—he snapped the chains from his wrists and smashed the shackles. No one was strong enough to subdue him. Day and night he wandered among the burial caves and in the hills, howling and cutting himself with sharp stones.

When Jesus was still some distance away, the man saw him, ran to meet him, and bowed low before him. With a shriek, he screamed, "Why are you interfering with me, Jesus, Son of the Most High God? In the name of God, I beg you, don't torture me!" For Jesus had already said to the spirit, "Come out of the man, you evil spirit."

Then Jesus demanded, "What is your name?"

And he replied, "My name is Legion, because there are many of us inside this man." Then the evil spirits begged him again and again not to send them to some distant place.

There happened to be a large herd of pigs feeding on the hillside nearby. "Send us into those pigs," the spirits begged. "Let us enter them."

So Jesus gave them permission. The evil spirits came out of the man and entered the pigs, and the entire herd of 2,000 pigs plunged down the steep hillside into the lake and drowned in the water.

The herdsmen fled to the nearby town and the surrounding countryside, spreading the news as they ran. People rushed out to see what had happened. A crowd soon gathered around Jesus, and they saw the man who had been possessed by the legion of demons. He was sitting there fully clothed and perfectly sane, and they were all afraid. (MARK 5:2–15 NLT; *also see* MATTHEW 8:28–34; LUKE 8:26–39)

A demon-possessed person can have supernatural strength and be compelled to harm self and others. One reason demons inhabit physical bodies is to attempt desecrating God's image within people. (There may well be a correlation between the number of demons involved and the seriousness of a problem.)

THE TWELVE PERFORM MIRACLES

[The twelve apostles told people] they should turn to God and change the way they think and act. They also forced many demons out of people and poured oil on many who were sick to cure them. (MARK 6:12–13 GOD'S WORD)

Miracles confirmed the divine authenticity of their call to repentance.

A NON-JEWISH WOMAN'S GREAT FAITH

A woman whose little daughter had an evil spirit heard about Jesus. She went to him and bowed down. The woman happened to be Greek, born in Phoenicia in Syria. She asked him to force the demon out of her daughter.

Jesus said to her, "First, let the children eat all they want. It's not right to take the children's food and throw it to the dogs."

She answered him, "Lord, even the dogs under the table eat some of the children's scraps."

Jesus said to her, "Because you have said this, go! The demon has left your daughter."

The woman went home and found the little child lying on her bed, and the demon was gone. (MARK 7:25–30 GOD'S WORD; *cf.* MATTHEW 15:21–28)

Even if rare, it's possible for children to be possessed. Jesus didn't need to be present to drive out demons, who afflicted Jews and Gentiles alike.

PREDICTING HIS OWN DEATH

[Jesus said] that the Son of Man must suffer many things and be rejected by the elders, chief priests and teachers of the law, and that he must be killed and after three days rise again. He spoke plainly about this, and Peter took him aside and began to rebuke him.

But when Jesus turned and looked at his disciples, he rebuked Peter. "Get behind me, Satan!" he said. "You do not have in mind the things of God, but merely human concerns" (MARK 8:31–33 NIV; *also see* MATTHEW 16:21–23).

Peter's attempt to dissuade Jesus from fulfilling God's plan of salvation made him a tempter not unlike the one Jesus had encountered in the desert.

—— RETURNING IN GLORY; ASHAMED OF HIS WORDS? ——

Whoever is ashamed of Me and My words in this adulterous and sinful generation, the Son of Man will also be ashamed of him when He comes in the glory of His Father with the holy angels. (MARK 8:38 NASB)

Angels will accompany Jesus when he returns in God's glory to judge the world (see Luke 9:26): "They shall all attend him, and minister to him, and add every thing they can to the luster of his appearance" (Matthew Henry).

———— DRIVING OUT DEMONS IN JESUS' NAME ————

"Teacher," said John, "we saw someone driving out demons in your name and we told him to stop, because he was not one of us."

"Do not stop him," Jesus said. "For no one who does a miracle in my name can in the next moment say anything bad about me, for whoever is not against us is for us" (MARK 9:38–40 NIV).

Possibly the apostles were upset by "outsider" success because they'd just seen failure (cf. Matthew 17:14–19; Mark 9:18; see below on Luke 9:37–42). Not being an apostle didn't negate his authority; he may have followed John the Baptist or been one of the dozens Jesus sent out (see Luke 10).

THE TIMING OF CHRIST'S RETURN

No one knows when that day or time will be, not the angels in heaven, not even the Son. Only the Father knows. (**MARK 13:32 NCV**)

Angels convey many divine secrets, but this information is kept from them.

APPEARING TO MARY MAGDALENE

When Jesus rose early on the first day of the week, he appeared first to Mary Magdalene, out of whom he had driven seven demons. (**MARK 16:9 NIV**)

Mary had been forgiven of much and also was given much, including the honor of being the first to see the risen Christ.

THE MIRACULOUS SIGNS OF BELIEVERS

These miraculous signs will accompany those who believe: They will cast out demons in my name, and they will speak in new languages. They will be able to handle snakes with safety, and if they drink anything poisonous, it won't hurt them. They will be able to place their hands on the sick, and they will be healed. (**MARK 16:17–18 NLT**)

Most say these powers were for Christians in that age only, to confirm the gospel's validity and establish the church. Exorcism is upheld or practiced in some branches of the faith, viewed with skepticism or disputed by others.

— GABRIEL FORETELLS THE BIRTH OF JOHN THE BAPTIST —

One day Zechariah was . . . chosen by lot to go into the Temple of the Lord and burn incense. . . . Then an angel of the Lord appeared . . . [and] when he saw the angel, Zechariah was startled and frightened. But the angel said to him, "Zechariah, don't be afraid. God has heard your prayer. Your wife, Elizabeth, will give birth to a son, and you will name him John. He will bring you joy and gladness, and many people will be happy because of his birth. John will be a great man for the Lord. He will never drink wine or beer, and even from birth, he will be filled with the Holy Spirit. He will help many people of Israel return to the Lord their God. He will go before the Lord in spirit and power like Elijah. He will make peace between parents and their children and will bring those who are not obeying God back to the right way of thinking, to make a people ready for the coming of the Lord."

Zechariah said to the angel, "How can I know that what you say is true? I am an old man, and my wife is old, too."

The angel answered him, "I am Gabriel. I stand before God, who sent me to talk to you and to tell you this good news. Now, listen! You will not be able to speak until the day these things happen, because you did not believe what I told you. But they will really happen" (LUKE 1:8–9, 11–20 NCV).

Gabriel (meaning "man of God") likely is the same angel who centuries earlier appeared to Daniel. Confirming trustworthiness, he revealed that he stands in God's presence. Zechariah's inability to speak probably was both punishment for unbelief and also further confirmation of the guarantee.

THE BIRTH OF JESUS FORETOLD

In the sixth month of Elizabeth's pregnancy, God sent the angel Gabriel to Nazareth . . . to a virgin pledged to be married to a man named Joseph, a descendant of David. The virgin's name was Mary. The angel went to her and said, "Greetings, you who are highly favored! The Lord is with you."

Mary was greatly troubled at his words and wondered what kind of greeting this might be. But the angel said to her, "Do not be afraid, Mary; you have found favor with God. You will conceive and give birth to a son, and you are to call him Jesus. He will be great and will be called the Son of the Most High. The Lord God will give him the throne of his father David, and he will reign over Jacob's descendents forever; his kingdom will never end."

"How will this be," Mary asked the angel, "since I am a virgin?"

The angel answered, "The Holy Spirit will come on you, and the power of the Most High will overshadow you. So the holy one to be born will be called the Son of God. Even Elizabeth your relative is going to have a child in her old age, and she who was said to be unable to conceive is in her sixth month. For no word from God will ever fail."

"I am the Lord's servant," Mary answered. "May your word to me be fulfilled." Then the angel left her. **(LUKE 1:26–38 NIV)**

Being sent with this message may suggest Gabriel's very high angelic rank.

—————— ANNOUNCING THE BIRTH OF JESUS ——————

There were in the same country shepherds abiding in the field, keeping watch over their flock by night.

And, lo, the angel of the Lord came upon them, and the glory of the Lord shone round about them: and they were sore afraid.

And the angel said unto them, Fear not: for, behold, I bring you good tidings of great joy, which shall be to all people.

For unto you is born this day in the city of David a Savior, which is Christ the Lord.

And this shall be a sign unto you; Ye shall find the babe wrapped in swaddling clothes, lying in a manger.

And suddenly there was with the angel a multitude of the heavenly host praising God, and saying,

Glory to God in the highest, and on earth peace, good will toward men.

And it came to pass, as the angels were gone away from them into heaven, the shepherds said one to another, Let us now go even unto Bethlehem, and see this thing which is come to pass, which the Lord hath made known unto us. (LUKE 2:8–15 KJV)

"Host" is heaven's angelic army. Showing God's glory and announcing his Son's birth to some of the least regarded members of society reflects Jesus' last-shall-be-first emphasis. In bringing "good tidings of great joy," the angel used the word meaning "to preach the good news."

—————— CARRYING OUT THE ANGEL'S INSTRUCTIONS ——————

Eight days after his birth, the child was circumcised and named Jesus. This was the name the angel had given him before his mother became pregnant. (LUKE 2:21 GOD'S WORD)

—————— Driving Out an Evil Spirit ——————

In the synagogue there was a man possessed by a demon, an impure spirit. He cried out at the top of his voice, "Go away! What do you want with us, Jesus of Nazareth? Have you come to destroy us? I know who you are—the Holy One of God!"

"Be quiet!" Jesus said sternly. "Come out of him!" Then the demon threw the man down before them all and came out without injuring him.

All the people were amazed and said to each other, "What words these are! With authority and power he gives orders to impure spirits and they come out!" (LUKE 4:33–36 NIV).

Techniques used by other exorcists included trying to scare out the demon and making the area around its host so unpleasant that the spirit, annoyed, would leave. People were impressed with Jesus' authoritative effectiveness.

—————— Commanding Demons to Be Silent ——————

Demons came out of many people, shouting, "You are the Son of God." But Jesus commanded the demons and would not allow them to speak, because they knew Jesus was the Christ. (LUKE 4:41 NCV)

It's not enough to know who Jesus is. We can know everything possible to know about him and still be fully committed to the devil's agenda.

—————— On John the Baptist and Demons ——————

John the Baptist has come eating no bread and drinking no wine, and [yet] you say, "He has a demon!" (LUKE 7:33 NASB).

It's possible that those to whom Jesus is speaking slandered John because they didn't want to heed his heaven-sent message of repentance.

────────── JESUS CURES A DEMON-POSSESSED BOY ──────────

A man in the crowd shouted, "Teacher, I beg you to look at my son. He's my only child. Whenever a spirit takes control of him, he shrieks, goes into convulsions, and foams at the mouth. After a struggle, the spirit goes away, leaving the child worn out. I begged your disciples to force the spirit out of him, but they couldn't do it."

Jesus answered, "You unbelieving and corrupt generation! How long must I be with you and put up with you? Bring your son here!"

While he was coming to Jesus, the demon knocked the boy to the ground and threw him into convulsions. Jesus ordered the evil spirit to leave. He cured the boy and gave him back to his father. (LUKE 9:38–42 GOD'S WORD; *also see* MATTHEW 17:14–19; MARK 9:17–29)

> *Demons can control a person's body; possession can resemble maladies like epilepsy or mental illness. Jesus had authorized and empowered the disciples (see Matthew 10:1) and expected them to successfully combat demons by their faith. But it was lacking, possibly through neglecting spiritual disciplines (e.g., prayer and fasting; see Matthew 17:21).*

────────── DEMONS OBEY THE DISCIPLES ──────────

When the seventy-two [disciples] came back, they were very happy and said, "Lord, even the demons obeyed us when we used your name!" Jesus said, "I saw Satan fall like lightning from heaven" (LUKE 10:17–18 NCV).

The name of Jesus brings victory over Satan. Some believe he was present when Satan and his demons were cast out of heaven. Others contend he's speaking about spiritual victories during the disciples' mission—that he saw Satan subsequently diminished as quickly as lightning flashes.

——— PUBLICLY (OPENLY) CONFESSING CHRIST ———

I tell you, all those who stand before others and say they believe in me, I, the Son of Man, will say before the angels of God that they belong to me. But all who stand before others and say they do not believe in me, I will say before the angels of God that they do not belong to me. **(LUKE 12:8–9 NCV)**

In judgment, at the world's end, whether or not Jesus acknowledges those who stand before him will determine which direction the angels take them.

——— HEALING A WOMAN ON THE SABBATH ———

Jesus was teaching in a synagogue on the day of worship. A woman who was possessed by a spirit was there. The spirit had disabled her for 18 years. She was hunched over and couldn't stand up straight. When Jesus saw her, he called her to come to him and said, "Woman, you are free from your disability." He placed his hands on her, and she immediately stood up straight and praised God.

The synagogue leader was irritated with Jesus for healing on the day of worship. [He] told the crowd, "There are six days when work can be done. So come on one of those days to be healed. Don't come on the day of worship."

The Lord said, "You hypocrites! Don't each of you free your ox or donkey on the day of worship? Don't you then take it out of its stall to give it some water to drink? Now, here is a descendant of Abraham. Satan has kept her in this condition for 18 years. Isn't it right to free her on [this day]?" . . . Everyone who opposed him felt ashamed. But the entire crowd was happy about the miraculous things he was doing. (LUKE 13:10–17 GOD'S WORD)

While it's wrong to attribute all physical ailments to spiritual circumstance, it's also wrong to believe health problems are never related to the work of demons. If a demon is involved, removal could bring immediate healing.

FORCING OUT DEMONS

Some Pharisees came to Jesus and said, "Go away from here! Herod wants to kill you!"

Jesus said to them, "Go tell that fox Herod, 'Today and tomorrow I am forcing demons out and healing people. Then, on the third day, I will reach my goal'" (LUKE 13:31–32 NCV).

Freeing people of spiritual affliction was integral to Jesus' ministry.

THE PARABLE OF THE LOST COIN

What woman, having ten silver coins, if she loses one coin, does not light a lamp, sweep the house, and search carefully until she finds it? And when she has found it, she calls her friends and neighbors together, saying, "Rejoice with me, for I have found the piece which I lost!" Likewise, I say to you, there is joy in the presence of the angels of God over one sinner who repents. (LUKE 15:8–10 NKJV)

Joy at a sinner's repentance is not on the part of angels but in their presence; God the Father, to whom each lost soul belongs, is rejoicing.

——————— THE RICH MAN AND LAZARUS ———————

Jesus tells of a rich man and a beggar (Lazarus) laid outside the rich man's gate. "Abraham's side" ("bosom") comes from the Jewish custom of reclining one's head near another's bosom during a meal. A person in such intimacy with Abraham implies he is in heaven and profoundly content.

The time came when the beggar died and the angels carried him to Abraham's side. The rich man also died and was buried. **(LUKE 16:22 NIV)**

Jewish writings indicate a belief that, after death, angels carried to heaven the souls of the righteous. By including this detail, Jesus seems to confirm this; many suggest it's realistic that the angels who ministered to people throughout their lives would also attend to them on their flight to heaven.

——————— PREPARING TO BETRAY JESUS ———————

The leading priests and teachers of the law were trying to find a way to kill Jesus, because they were afraid of the people.

Satan entered Judas Iscariot, one of Jesus' twelve apostles. Judas went to the leading priests and some of the soldiers who guarded the Temple and talked to them about a way to hand Jesus over to them. **(LUKE 22:2–4 NCV)**

Never having been a true Christ-follower explains how Satan encouraged Judas' greed and other evil intentions. As to why Satan would prompt him toward a result that led to Christ's sacrifice, Satan possesses supernatural abilities yet still has limited knowledge of the future. He may also lack wisdom or self-control to foresee or consider the effects of his actions.

—————— JESUS PREDICTS PETER'S DENIAL ——————

Simon, Simon, Satan has asked to test all of you as a farmer sifts his wheat. I have prayed that you will not lose your faith! Help your brothers be stronger when you come back to me. (LUKE 22:31–32 NCV)

> *Satan wanted to test and shake down the disciples to see whether he could cause them to be "blown away." The text implies Satan needed permission.*

—————— PRAYING IN THE GARDEN OF GETHSEMANE ——————

"Father, if it is your will, take this cup of suffering away from me. However, your will must be done, not mine." Then an angel from heaven appeared to him and gave him strength. (LUKE 22:42–43 GOD'S WORD)

> *The angel appeared, in response, to strengthen and encourage Jesus so his human nature could withstand the coming physical and mental anguish.*

—————— REPORTING ANGELS' TESTIMONY TO THE DISCIPLES ——————

Some of the women from our group startled us. They went to the tomb early this morning and didn't find his body. They told us that they had seen angels who said that he's alive. (LUKE 24:22–23 GOD'S WORD)

—————— JESUS CALLS PHILIP AND NATHANAEL ——————

You believe because I told you I saw you under the fig tree. You will see greater things than that. . . . You will see heaven open,

and the angels of God ascending and descending on the Son of
Man. (JOHN 1:50–51 NIV)

Alluding to Jacob's ladder (Genesis 28:12), Jesus says he's the con-
nection between heaven and earth. Many view angels' ascending/
descending "on Jesus" as a metaphor showing him as the way between
God and people.

─────────── **A DISCIPLE, A BETRAYER, A DEVIL** ───────────

Jesus said, "I chose the twelve of you, but one is a devil." He
was speaking of Judas . . . who would later betray him. (JOHN
6:70–71 NLT)

Judas lived out the meaning of "devil," acting as adversary, slan-
derer, and false accuser and agreeing with the deceivers that Jesus
deserved arrest.

─────────── **ACCUSED OF BEING DEMON-POSSESSED** ───────────

[Jesus said to the Jews,] "Has not Moses given you the law? Yet
not one of you keeps the law. Why are you trying to kill me?"
   "You are demon-possessed," the crowd answered. "Who is
trying to kill you?" (JOHN 7:19–20 NIV).

Demoniacs often were thought to be lunatics who had no idea what
they were saying. These accusers likely thought Jesus was being para-
noid, unaware that the Jewish leaders actively were plotting to kill him.

─────────── **CHILDREN OF THE DEVIL** ───────────

Jesus is addressing Jewish leaders and others who are insisting that
they're children of Abraham and that God is their Father.

If you are Abraham's children, do the deeds of Abraham. But as it is, you are seeking to kill Me, a man who has told you the truth, which I heard from God; this Abraham did not do. You are doing the deeds of your father. . . . If God were your Father, you would love Me. . . . [But] you are of your father the devil, and you want to do the desires of your father. He was a murderer from the beginning, and does not stand in the truth because there is no truth in him. Whenever he speaks a lie, he speaks from his own nature, for he is a liar and the father of lies. (JOHN 8:39–42, 44 NASB)

——— ACCUSED OF BEING DEMON-POSSESSED ———

The Jews replied to Jesus, "Aren't we right when we say that you're a Samaritan and that you're possessed by a demon?"

Jesus answered, "I'm not possessed. I honor my Father, but you dishonor me. I don't want my own glory. But there is someone who wants it, and he is the judge. I can guarantee this truth: Whoever obeys what I say will never see death."

The Jews told Jesus, "Now we know that you're possessed by a demon. Abraham died, and so did the prophets, but you say, 'Whoever does what I say will never taste death.' Are you greater than our father Abraham, who died? The prophets have also died. Who do you think you are?"

Jesus said, "If I bring glory to myself, my glory is nothing. My Father is the one who gives me glory, and you say that he is your God. Yet, you haven't known him. However, I know him. If I would say that I didn't know him, I would be a liar like all of you. But I do know him, and I do what he says" (JOHN 8:48–55 GOD's WORD).

Jesus cites ways he's unlike those who are demon-possessed: He honors his Father, he doesn't seek his own glory, he knows God, he obeys God.

——————— DISAGREEING ABOUT JESUS ———————

A division occurred again among the Jews because of [Jesus'] words. Many of them were saying, "He has a demon and is insane. Why do you listen to Him?" Others were saying, "These are not the sayings of one demon-possessed. A demon cannot open the eyes of the blind, can he?" (JOHN 10:19–21 NASB).

Jesus had just said that he is the good shepherd who will lay down his life for his sheep and will take back his life again. Regarding the people's disagreement, demons don't exhibit love, compassion, or any other virtue. Jesus' miracles not only reveal who he is but also who he isn't.

——————— A VOICE FROM HEAVEN ———————

"My soul is troubled, and what shall I say? 'Father, save Me from this hour'? But for this purpose I came to this hour. Father, glorify Your name."

Then a voice came from heaven, saying, "I have both glorified it and will glorify it again."

. . . The people who stood by and heard it said that it had thundered. Others said, "An angel has spoken to Him" (JOHN 12:27–29 NKJV).

The text doesn't clarify whether the audible heavenly voice was God the Father or an angel speaking on his behalf. Opinions vary as to why some in the crowd heard a voice while others heard only a sound like thunder.

——————— THE LAST SUPPER ———————

Jesus and his followers were at the evening meal. The devil had already persuaded Judas Iscariot . . . to turn against Jesus. (JOHN 13:2 NCV)

Satan couldn't force Judas to betray Jesus—he only could offer the temptation. In Judas, though, Satan found a heart predisposed toward yielding to sin, especially if money was involved.

--------------------- TAKING THE BREAD ---------------------

"I will dip this bread into the dish. The man I give it to is the man who will turn against me." So Jesus took a piece of bread, dipped it, and gave it to Judas. . . . As soon as Judas took the bread, Satan entered him. Jesus said to him, "The thing that you will do—do it quickly" (JOHN 13:26-27 NCV).

Judas rejected a last chance to refuse betrayal; Satan took full possession.

--------------------- THE EMPTY TOMB ---------------------

Mary was standing outside the tomb crying, and as she wept, she stooped and looked in. She saw two white-robed angels, one sitting at the head and the other at the foot of the place where the body of Jesus had been lying. "Dear woman, why are you crying?" they asked her. "Because they have taken away my Lord," she replied, "and I don't know where they have put him" (JOHN 20:11-13 NLT; *also see* MATTHEW 28:1-7; MARK 16:1-8; LUKE 24:1-8).

The angels' position in the tomb elicits the image of the golden cherubim atop the mercy seat (Exodus 25:17-19). Formerly, sins were covered symbolically with sprinkled animal blood; the risen Jesus is the new mercy seat, whereby sin's price has been paid through his blood. (Luke and John mention two angelic beings; Matthew and Mark mention one. The apparent discrepancy is the result of their selection of which details to include. Also, it's not uncommon for the spokesman at an event to be noted while one companion [or more] is unmentioned.)

6

Angels and Demons
in Acts and the Epistles

~~~

Acts provides an historical account of the church's founding, the spreading of the gospel from Jerusalem throughout the Roman empire, and the persecution believers encountered. The twenty-one epistles (apostolic letters to churches or individuals) also provide details about the church's early days, elaborating on key tenets, correcting false teachings, and encouraging believers.

THE DECEIT AND DEATH OF ANANIAS

A man named Ananias and his wife Sapphira sold some property. They agreed to hold back some of the money they had pledged and turned only part of it over to the apostles.

Peter asked, "Ananias, why did you let Satan fill you with the idea that you could deceive the Holy Spirit? You've held back some of the money you received for the land. While you had the land, it was your own. After it was sold, you could have done as you pleased with the money. So how could you do a thing like this? You didn't lie to people but to God!"

When Ananias heard Peter say this, he dropped dead. Everyone who heard about his death was terrified. (ACTS 5:1–5 GOD'S WORD)

"Whatever Satan might suggest, he could not have filled Ananias' heart with this wickedness had he not been consenting" (Matthew Henry).

———— APOSTLES IMPRISONED AND RELEASED ————

The high priest and his officials . . . were filled with jealousy. They arrested the apostles and put them in the public jail. But an angel of the Lord came at night, opened the gates . . . and brought them out. Then he told them, "Go to the Temple and give the people this message of life!" (ACTS 5:17–20 NLT).

The purposes for the angel's miracle included demonstrating to others the truth of the gospel, encouraging the apostles and strengthening their faith, and expressly, enabling them to fulfill the command to speak at the temple.

———————— THE ARREST OF STEPHEN ————————

Synagogue members began to argue with Stephen, a godly man. Unable to match his wisdom, they furtively persuaded others to accuse him falsely, of blasphemy, then had him hauled before the Jewish high court (Sanhedrin).

All the people in the meeting were watching Stephen closely and saw that his face looked like the face of an angel. (ACTS 6:15 NCV)

Some believe his "angelic" face displayed confidence and peace. Others suggest it was radiant, as God's glory dwelling in him showed on his face.

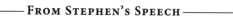

FROM STEPHEN'S SPEECH

An angel appeared to Moses in the flames of a burning bush. . . . This is the same Moses whom [the Israelites] had rejected with the words, "Who made you ruler and judge?" He was sent to be their ruler and deliverer by God himself, through the angel who appeared to him. . . . He was in the assembly in the wilderness, with the angel who spoke to him on Mount Sinai, and with our ancestors; and he received living words to pass on to us. . . . [But] was there ever a prophet your ancestors did not persecute? They even killed those who predicted the coming of the Righteous One. And now you have betrayed and murdered him—you who have received the law that was given through angels but have not obeyed it. (ACTS 7:30, 35, 38, 52–53 NIV)

Angels were said to have intermediated at Sinai (see Galatians 3:19).

PHILIP TELLS AN ETHIOPIAN ABOUT JESUS

An angel of the Lord spoke to Philip, saying, "Arise and go toward the south along the road which goes down from Jerusalem to Gaza." This is desert. So he arose and went. And behold, a man of Ethiopia, a eunuch of great authority under Candace the queen of the Ethiopians, who had charge of all her treasury, and had come to Jerusalem to worship, was returning. And sitting in his chariot, he was reading Isaiah the prophet. Then the Spirit said to Philip, "Go near and overtake this chariot."

So Philip ran to him, and heard him reading the prophet Isaiah, and said, "Do you understand what you are reading?"

And he said, "How can I, unless someone guides me?" And he asked Philip to come up and sit with him. (ACTS 8:26–31 NKJV)

An angel could have told the Ethiopian how to be saved, but God has entrusted that responsibility to his people, contends Warren Wiersbe: "Angels have never personally experienced God's grace; therefore, they can never bear witness of what it means to be saved."

CORNELIUS SENDS FOR PETER

One afternoon about three o'clock, Cornelius clearly saw a vision. An angel of God came to him and said, "Cornelius!"

Cornelius stared at the angel. He became afraid and said, "What do you want, Lord?"

The angel said, "God has heard your prayers. He has seen that you give to the poor, and he remembers you. Send some men now to Joppa to bring back a man named Simon who is also called Peter. He is staying with a man, also named Simon, who is a tanner and has a house beside the sea." When the angel . . . left, Cornelius called two of his servants and a soldier . . . [and] explained everything to them and sent them to Joppa. . . .

[Later, Cornelius explained to Peter what had taken place.] "Four days ago, I was praying in my house at this same time— three o'clock in the afternoon. Suddenly, there was a man standing before me wearing shining clothes. He said, 'Cornelius, God has heard your prayer and has seen that you give to the poor and remembers you'" (ACTS 10:3–8, 30–31 NCV).

This revelation came through a vision (not a dream or a trance); the angel (who looked like a radiantly clothed man) assuaged Cornelius' fear by assuring him that God heard his prayer and knew the details of his life. Cornelius was still praying when the angel said he'd been heard. Perhaps he asked God how to be saved, since that's what Peter shared.

PETER TESTIFIES ABOUT JESUS

You know of Jesus of Nazareth, how God anointed Him with the Holy Spirit and with power, and how He went about doing good and healing all who were oppressed by the devil, for God was with Him. (ACTS 10:38 NASB)

PETER'S MIRACULOUS ESCAPE FROM PRISON

On the very night when Herod was about to bring him forward, Peter was sleeping between two soldiers, bound with two chains, and guards in front of the door were watching over the prison. And behold, an angel of the Lord suddenly appeared and a light shone in the cell; and he struck Peter's side and woke him up, saying, "Get up quickly." And his chains fell off his hands. And the angel said to him, "Gird yourself and put on your sandals." And he did so. And he said to him, "Wrap your cloak around you and follow me." And he went out and continued to follow, and he did not know that what was being done by the angel was real, but thought he was seeing a vision. When they had passed the first and second guard, they came to the iron gate that leads into the city, which opened for them by itself; and they went out and went along one street, and immediately the angel departed from him. When Peter came to himself, he said, "Now I know for sure that the Lord has sent forth His angel and rescued me from the hand of Herod and from all that the Jewish people were expecting" (ACTS 12:6–11 NASB).

The angel had no trouble getting Peter out of chains, past guards, or through iron. Some suggest the light in the cell emanated from him and was the Lord's glory. The rescue was an answer to prayer; the church had been praying for Peter "earnestly" or "fervently" or "constantly" (v. 5).

PETER MISTAKEN FOR AN ANGEL

Peter knocked at the outer entrance, and a servant named Rhoda came to answer the door. When she recognized Peter's voice, she was so overjoyed she ran back without opening it and exclaimed, "Peter is at the door!"

"You're out of your mind," they told her. When she kept insisting that it was so, they said, "It must be his angel."

But Peter kept on knocking, and when they opened the door and saw him, they were astonished. (ACTS 12:13–16 NIV)

Many Jews believed that every person had a guardian angel. This passage is thought to be an example of that belief, though not proof of its truth.

AN ANGEL STRIKES DOWN HEROD AGRIPPA

Herod, arrayed in royal apparel, sat on his throne and gave an oration. . . . And the people kept shouting, "The voice of a god and not of a man!" Then immediately an angel of the Lord struck him, because he did not give glory to God. And he was eaten by worms and died. (ACTS 12:21–23 NKJV)

PAUL CONFRONTS A SORCERER

A governor had invited Barnabas and Saul [Paul] to tell him about God's word. But his sorcerer kept interfering, urging him not to listen.

[Paul] was filled with the Holy Spirit, and he looked the sorcerer in the eye. Then he said, "You son of the devil, full of every sort of deceit and fraud, and enemy of all that is good! Will you never stop perverting the true ways of the Lord? Watch now, for the Lord has laid his hand of punishment upon you, and you will be struck blind. You will not see the sunlight for some time." Instantly mist and darkness came over the man's eyes, and he began groping around begging for someone to take his hand and lead him.

When the governor saw what had happened, he became a believer, for he was astonished at the teaching about the Lord. (ACTS 13:9–12 NLT)

In calling the sorcerer the devil's child, Paul meant his false messages about God are like those one would expect from his spiritual father.

Using Jesus' Name to Cast Out Evil Spirits

Some Jews used to travel from place to place and force evil spirits out of people. They tried to use the name of the Lord Jesus to force evil spirits out of those who were possessed. These Jews would say, "I order you to come out in the name of Jesus, whom Paul talks about." Seven sons of Sceva, a Jewish chief priest, were doing this.

But the evil spirit answered them, "I know Jesus, and I'm acquainted with Paul, but who are you?" Then the man possessed by the evil spirit attacked them. He beat them up so badly that they ran out of that house naked and wounded. (ACTS 19:13–16 GOD'S WORD)

These exorcists, noting Paul's success, thought invoking the Lord's name would yield the same results. Demons recognize imposters, counterfeits; confronting them without God's power and authority can be hazardous.

———————— **PAUL BEFORE THE SANHEDRIN** ————————

Sadducees say that there is no resurrection—and no angel or spirit; but the Pharisees confess both. Then there arose a loud outcry. And the scribes of the Pharisees' party arose and protested, saying, "We find no evil in this man; but if a spirit or an angel has spoken to him, let us not fight against God" (**ACTS 23:8–9 NKJV**).

——**PAUL RECOUNTS JESUS' WORDS AT HIS CONVERSION**——

I will deliver you from the [Jews and] the Gentiles, to whom I now send you, to open their eyes . . . to turn them from darkness to light, and from the power of Satan to God, that they may receive forgiveness of sins and an inheritance among those who are sanctified by faith in Me. (**ACTS 26:17–18 NKJV**)

Satan has power over people when he keeps them in the dark, where they are blinded to the light of God (Jamieson-Fausset-Brown).

——— **PAUL TRUSTS IN GOD DURING A STORM AT SEA** ———

Last night an angel of the God to whom I belong and whom I serve stood beside me and said, "Do not be afraid, Paul. You must stand trial before Caesar; and God has graciously given you the lives of all who sail with you." So keep up your courage, men, for I have faith in God that it will happen just as he told me. (**ACTS 27:23–25 NIV**)

——— WHAT CAN SEPARATE US FROM GOD'S LOVE? ———

Nothing can ever separate us from God's love. Neither death nor life, neither angels nor demons, neither our fears for today nor our worries about tomorrow—not even the powers of hell. (ROMANS 8:38 NLT)

Many believe "angels" refers to demons/evil angels, as good angels by nature wouldn't try to do this. Others say it applies to all angels: "The good angels will not, the bad shall not; and neither can. The good angels are engaged friends, the bad are restrained enemies" (Matthew Henry).

——— PAUL'S CLOSING WORDS TO THE CHURCH IN ROME ———

The God of peace will soon crush Satan under your feet.
The grace of our Lord Jesus be with you. (ROMANS 16:20 NASB)

This likely refers to God's promise that the serpent who deceived Adam and Eve would one day be crushed beneath the feet of her seed (Genesis 3:15).

——— ON BEING AN APOSTLE OF CHRIST ———

God has displayed us, the apostles, last, as men condemned to death; for we have been made a spectacle to the world, both to angels and to men. (1 CORINTHIANS 4:9 NKJV)

Paul probably is likening the apostles' public humiliation to the Roman practice of putting prisoners in an amphitheater to fight to the death.

——— REBUKING IMMORALITY IN THE CHURCH ———

Paul comments on a man in the church having taken his father's wife.

When you meet together in the name of our Lord Jesus, and I meet with you in spirit with the power of our Lord Jesus, then hand this man over to Satan. So his sinful self will be destroyed, and his spirit will be saved on the day of the Lord. (1 CORINTHIANS 5:4–5 NCV)

"Hand over to Satan" means expelling an unrepentant member, letting him experience the consequences of pleasing the fleshly nature. Once he's had enough, the sinful impulse might be overrun and his spirit could be saved.

—— AVOIDING LAWSUITS WITH OTHER CHRISTIANS ——

Don't you realize that we will judge angels? So you should surely be able to resolve ordinary disputes in this life. (1 CORINTHIANS 6:3 NLT)

Believers will judge fallen angels, not those who remained faithful to God.

———— SEXUAL CONNECTION IN MARRIAGE ————

Do not refuse to give your bodies to each other, unless you both agree to stay away from sexual relations for a time so you can give your time to prayer. Then come together again so Satan cannot tempt you because of a lack of self-control. (1 CORIN-THIANS 7:5 NCV)

Married couples are better able to maintain self-control and resist temptation when they regularly satisfy each other's appetites.

———— WARNINGS FROM ISRAEL'S HISTORY ————

Do not grumble, as some of them did—and were killed by the destroying angel. (1 CORINTHIANS 10:10 NIV)

Paul apparently refers to opponents of Moses and Aaron (see Numbers 16).

SACRIFICES TO DEMONS

These sacrifices are offered to demons [false gods], not to God. And I don't want you to participate with demons. You cannot drink from the cup of the Lord and from the cup of demons, too. You cannot eat at the Lord's Table and at the table of demons, too. **(1 CORINTHIANS 10:20–21 NLT)**

While false gods are powerless, demons take advantage of idol worship to deceive people and keep them from knowing the true God.

ON BEING UNDER AUTHORITY

Man did not come from woman, but woman came from man. And man was not made for woman, but woman was made for man. So that is why a woman should have a symbol of authority on her head, because of the angels. **(1 CORINTHIANS 11:8–10 NCV)**

In that culture, a woman's hair was an object of male lust; an uncovered head in public was a sign of disrespect for her husband. Some say because "the angels" were present whenever believers gathered, it was important that women not subject them to something seen as offensive. Others suggest a woman's head covering is a sign of her authority; because woman has her origin in man (Genesis 2) she reflects his glory; by covering her head in worship she conceals his glory and is prepared to reflect God's. Others maintain that the covering signifies a woman's recognition of authority over her. Some say covering an "unclean" head correlates to the angels in God's presence who use their wings to cover their faces and feet (Isaiah 6).

─────── On Speaking With "Tongues of Angels" ───────

If I speak with the tongues of men and of angels, but do not have love, I have become a noisy gong or a clanging cymbal. **(1 CORINTHIANS 13:1 NASB)**

Scripture indicates that angels understand and speak human languages. Here, Paul may be saying they have their own special language—or he may be using hyperbole. Some believe "tongues of angels" refers to the New Testament gift of tongues still upheld or practiced in some churches.

─────── Forgiveness for the One Who Sins ───────

When you forgive this man, I forgive him, too. And when I forgive whatever needs to be forgiven, I do so with Christ's authority for your benefit, so that Satan will not outsmart us. For we are familiar with his evil schemes. **(2 CORINTHIANS 2:10–11 NLT)**

When a believer has sinned and needs forgiveness from others, Satan can seek to demoralize him by implying his situation to be hopeless or creating disunity within the church, bringing dishonor upon the gospel message.

─────── "False Apostles" ───────

False apostles . . . are deceitful workers who disguise themselves as apostles of Christ. But I am not surprised! Even Satan disguises himself as an angel of light. **(2 CORINTHIANS 11:13–14 NLT)**

The deceiver is adept at using appearances to conceal his true identity.

——————— Paul's Impairment ———————

So that I would not become too proud of the wonderful things that were shown to me, a painful physical problem, . . . a messenger from Satan [was] sent to beat me and keep me from being too proud. **(2 CORINTHIANS 12:7 NCV)**

God allowed Satan to afflict Paul in some way to keep him humble.

——————— A Curse on Anyone Preaching ———————
a Different Gospel

Whoever tells you good news that is different from the Good News we gave you should be condemned to hell, even if he is one of us or an angel from heaven. **(GALATIANS 1:8 GOD'S WORD)**

Rather than a heavenly angel possibly preaching falsely, Paul likely used strong rhetoric to emphasize the threat posed by deceivers/ false teachers.

——————— The Purpose of the Law ———————

[The law] was given to show that the wrong things people do are against God's will. And it continued until the special descendant [Jesus], who had been promised, came. The law was given through angels who used Moses for a mediator to give the law to people. **(GALATIANS 3:19 NCV)**

Though the Old Testament doesn't mention angels participating in the giving of the law, Paul says they were mediators between God and Moses.

——————— The Galatians' Love for Paul ———————

Even though my illness was a trial to you, you did not treat me with contempt or scorn. Instead, you welcomed me as if I were an angel of God, as if I were Christ Jesus himself. **(GALATIANS 4:14 NIV)**

Being received with highest respect is "welcome worthy of an angel."

——————— The Former Condition of Believers ———————

You used to live in sin, just like the rest of the world, obeying the devil—the commander of the powers in the unseen world. He is the spirit at work in the hearts of those who refuse to obey God. **(EPHESIANS 2:2 NLT)**

Satan, ruler of the evil spirits, isn't personally at work in every unbeliever. As a created being, he can't be everywhere at once; his influence usually is indirect. Those not doing what God says are carrying out Satan's orders.

——————— Living as Children of Light ———————

Don't give the devil any opportunity to work. **(EPHESIANS 4:27 GOD'S WORD)**

Satan waits to get a foot in the door. If people give in to evil desires and accept sin, he can exploit their choices to create divisions among believers.

——————— Being Ready for Spiritual Conflict ———————

Put on the whole armor of God, that ye may be able to stand against the wiles of the devil.

For we wrestle not against flesh and blood, but against principalities, against powers, against the rulers of the darkness of this world, against spiritual wickedness in high places. **(EPHESIANS 6:11–12 KJV)**

> *Satan schemes to ensnare and enslave, to distract people with the world's cares and entice them by appealing to fleshly appetites. No one should attempt to stand against him without having first put in place spiritual "protective gear" (see vv. 13–17). Christians' real enemies aren't other people but the unseen forces of darkness opposing what God wants to accomplish in people's lives.*

— JESUS' TRIUMPH OVER "POWERS AND AUTHORITIES" —

Having disarmed the powers and authorities, he made a public spectacle of them, triumphing over them by the cross. **(COLOSSIANS 2:15 NIV)**

> *Some believe "powers and authorities" refers to evil angels or demonic spirits. Others suggest they were the Jewish religious leaders.*

— FREEDOM FROM ARTIFICIAL REQUIREMENTS —

Do not let anyone who delights in false humility and the worship of angels disqualify you. Such a person also goes into great detail about what they have seen; they are puffed up with idle notions by their unspiritual mind. **(COLOSSIANS 2:18 NIV)**

> *Paul warns about Gnostics, some of whom sought notice for "humility," under which pretext they feigned being unworthy to go directly to God and worshiped angels instead. Believers are to stay connected to Christ.*

——— Longing to Visit the Thessalonians ———

We wanted very much to come to you, and I, Paul, tried again and again, but Satan prevented us. (1 THESSALONIANS 2:18 NLT)

> *Satan's undefined interference showed limited understanding of the future. Many scholars believe 1 Thessalonians was Paul's earliest letter to a church; David Guzik suggests that by hindering Paul from traveling, Satan got him into a habit that subsequently has spoken to billions of people.*

——— Concern for the Thessalonians' Faith ———

Even when we were with you, we told you we all would have to suffer, and you know it has happened. Because of this, when I could wait no longer, I sent Timothy to you so I could learn about your faith. I was afraid the devil had tempted you, and perhaps our hard work would have been wasted. (1 THESSALONIANS 3:4–5 NCV)

> *Satan seeks to destroy faith. If he can entice Christians to doubt God, he can deconstruct the hard work of God's servants in building his kingdom.*

——— Relief at Christ's Return ———

It is also right for God to give all of us relief from our suffering. He will do this when the Lord Jesus is revealed, coming from heaven with his mighty angels in a blazing fire. (2 THESSALONIANS 1:7 GOD'S WORD)

> *Some think this refers to a class of angels, of exalted rank, given special power to fulfill God's will. Others note that Paul says "Jesus' angels"; he's their creator, the rightful object of their worship and*

112

adoration. *The Greek calls them the "angels of his might," i.e., the angels by whom he makes his power and authority recognized (Jamieson-Fausset-Brown).*

"THE MAN OF SIN"

The man of sin will come with the power of Satan. He will use every kind of power, including miraculous and wonderful signs. But they will be lies. **(2 THESSALONIANS 2:9 GOD'S WORD)**

Some identify this Satan-empowered "man of sin" ("lawlessness") as the antichrist (see Revelation). Others associate him with a Roman emperor.

STAYING FAITHFUL

Continue to have faith and do what you know is right. Some people have rejected this, and their faith has been shipwrecked. Hymenaeus and Alexander have done that, and I have given them to Satan so they will learn not to speak against God. **(1 TIMOTHY 1:19–20 NCV; *see above,* on 1 CORINTHIANS 5:4–5)**

GUIDELINES FOR CHURCH LEADERS

An elder must not be a new believer, because he might become proud, and the devil would cause him to fall. Also, people outside the church must speak well of him so that he will not be disgraced and fall into the devil's trap. **(1 TIMOTHY 3:6–7 NLT)**

The accuser would exploit flaws or inconsistencies in an elder to undermine his credibility and effectiveness.

The Great Mystery

Without question, this is the great mystery of our faith:
Christ was revealed in a human body
and vindicated by the Spirit.
He was seen by angels
and announced to the nations.
He was believed in throughout the world
and taken to heaven in glory. **(1 TIMOTHY 3:16 NLT)**

Warnings Against Apostasy and Deception

The Spirit clearly says that in later times some will abandon the faith and follow deceiving spirits and things taught by demons. **(1 TIMOTHY 4:1 NIV)**

As an imitator of God, Satan seeks to use his doctrine to deceive believers into giving up on their faith; sometimes he uses ministers and teachers in churches to spread his lies (Warren Wiersbe).

Advice About Widows

I counsel younger widows to marry, to have children, to manage their homes and to give the enemy no opportunity for slander. Some have in fact already turned away to follow Satan. **(1 TIMOTHY 5:14–15 NIV)**

Paul encourages young widows to remarry, to concern themselves with and invest in family life, so that the devil will have no grounds to accuse.

—————————— CONCERNING ELDERS ——————————

I charge you before God and the Lord Jesus Christ and the elect angels that you observe these things without prejudice, doing nothing with partiality. (1 TIMOTHY 5:21 NKJV)

"Elect angels" refers to God's chosen angels, not the fallen angels.

—————— MORE ADVICE REGARDING ELDERS ——————

The Lord's servant must gently teach those who disagree. Then maybe God will let them change their minds so they can accept the truth. And they may wake up and escape from the trap of the devil, who catches them to do what he wants. (2 TIMOTHY 2:25–26 NCV)

—————— GOD'S SON IS SUPERIOR TO THE ANGELS ——————

[Jesus was] made so much better than the angels, as he hath by inheritance obtained a more excellent name than they. For unto which of the angels said [God] at any time, Thou art my Son, this day have I begotten thee? And again, I will be to him a Father, and he shall be to me a Son? And again, when he bringeth in the firstbegotten into the world, he saith, And let all the angels of God worship him. And of the angels he saith, [he] maketh his angels spirits, and his ministers a flame of fire. . . . To which of the angels said he at any time, Sit [at] my right hand, until I make thine enemies thy footstool? Are they not all ministering spirits, sent forth to minister for them who shall be heirs of salvation? (HEBREWS 1:4–7, 13–14 KJV)

The writer of Hebrews emphasizes Christ's status and worthiness because some people were worshiping angels instead (see comments

115

on Colossians 2:18). In God's kingdom, Jesus has placement of highest privilege; angels (spirits who can assume human form) are God's servants to humans.

Angels as Intermediaries

The message God delivered through angels has always stood firm, and every violation of the law and every act of disobedience was punished. **(HEBREWS 2:2 NLT; *also see comments on* GALATIANS 3:19)**

Angels and the World to Come

It is not angels who will control the future world. **(HEBREWS 2:5 NLT)**

God will not place angels in authority when Christ establishes his kingdom.

Christ Became Like Humans

"You made him a little lower than the angels. You crowned him with glory and honor. You put everything under his control." When God put everything under his Son's control, nothing was left out. However, at the present time we still don't see everything under his Son's control. Jesus was made a little lower than the angels, but we see him crowned with glory and honor because he suffered death. Through God's kindness he died on behalf of everyone. **(HEBREWS 2:7–9 GOD'S WORD)**

While taking on human form did for a time make Jesus "a little lower than the angels," he's now glorified and honored at God's right hand. To his divinity, Jesus added humanity; he was never an angel.

──────── **DESTROYING SATAN'S HOLD ON DEATH** ────────

Since the children are made of flesh and blood, it's logical that the Savior took on flesh and blood in order to rescue them by his death. By embracing death, taking it into himself, he destroyed the Devil's hold on death and freed all who cower through life, scared to death of death. It's obvious, of course, that he didn't go to all this trouble for angels. It was for people like us, children of Abraham. **(HEBREWS 2:14–16 THE MESSAGE)**

> *His "hold on death" lay in being the author of sin (John 8:44); sin brings death (Romans 6:23). Jesus didn't become an angel or die to save angels: "He stooped lower than the angels to become a man!" (Warren Wiersbe).*

──────────── **THE HEAVENLY JERUSALEM** ────────────

You have come to Mount Zion and to the city of the living God, the heavenly Jerusalem, to an innumerable company of angels. **(HEBREWS 12:22 NKJV)**

> *There are more angels in heaven than we can count.*

──────────── **SHOWING HOSPITALITY** ────────────

Do not neglect to show hospitality to strangers, for by this some have entertained angels without knowing it. **(HEBREWS 13:2 NASB)**

> *This primarily stresses the importance of hospitality, but some have thought they were hosting strangers and later realized they'd welcomed angels.*

——————— **FAITH AND WORKS** ———————

You believe that there is one God. You do well. Even the demons believe—and tremble! (JAMES 2:19 NKJV)

Knowing truth isn't enough. What we do with what we know is what counts.

——————— **TWO KINDS OF "WISDOM"** ———————

Are there those among you who are truly wise and understanding? Then they should show it by living right and doing good things with a gentleness that comes from wisdom. But if you are selfish and have bitter jealousy in your hearts, do not brag. Your bragging is a lie that hides the truth. That kind of "wisdom" does not come from God but from the world. It is not spiritual; it is from the devil. (JAMES 3:13–15 NCV)

The "wisdom" Satan imparts isn't wisdom at all. Applying the devil's ideology produces selfishness, envy, boasting, and deceit.

——————— **SURRENDERING TO GOD, RESISTING SATAN** ———————

Submit yourselves therefore to God. Resist the devil, and he will flee from you. (JAMES 4:7 KJV)

We oppose the devil by giving ourselves to God. When we're fully submitted, leaving nothing withheld, Satan has no place or prerogative.

——————— **THE GOSPEL SHOWN THROUGH THE PROPHETS** ———————

What the prophets had spoken, the Holy Spirit, who was sent from heaven, has now made known to you by those who spread the Good News. . . . These are things that even the angels want to look into. **(1 PETER 1:12 GOD's WORD)**

Angels "stoop and look intently" at God's great plan entering fulfillment.

─────────── CHRIST'S PLACE OF HONOR ───────────

Christ . . . is seated in the place of honor next to God, and all the angels and authorities and powers accept his authority. **(1 PETER 3:22 NLT)**

Jesus has authority over all angels, both the good and the bad.

─────────── BEWARE OF SATAN ───────────

Be of sober spirit, be on the alert. Your adversary, the devil, prowls around like a roaring lion, seeking someone to devour. But resist him, firm in your faith, knowing that the same experiences of suffering are being accomplished by your brethren who are in the world. **(1 PETER 5:8-9 NASB)**

Satan is intent on destroying people's spiritual well-being. Warren Wiersbe advises that while believers shouldn't underestimate his ability to inflict suffering, neither should they blame him for each headache or flat tire.

─────────── THE FATE OF FALLEN ANGELS ───────────

God did not spare even the angels who sinned. He threw them into hell, in gloomy pits of darkness, where they are being held until the day of judgment. **(2 PETER 2:4 NLT)**

Some say Peter speaks of the rebellion against God by the angel who became Satan with a third of God's angels (now demons); they were cast from heaven (see Revelation 12). Others contend this wouldn't explain how Satan/demons roam the earth while other demons are locked up; they posit this latter group as having committed another horrific sin warranting permanent detention, citing an event (see Genesis 6:2) in which "sons of God" married "daughters of men," supposing these to be angels and human women. Critics say such relationships are impossible and that "sons of God" in Scripture sometimes refers to people.

THE FOOLISHNESS OF FALSE TEACHERS

The Lord knows how to rescue godly people from their trials, even while keeping the wicked under punishment until the day of final judgment. He is especially hard on those who follow their own twisted sexual desire, and who despise authority.

These people are proud and arrogant, daring even to scoff at supernatural beings without so much as trembling. But the angels, who are far greater in power and strength, do not dare to bring from the Lord a charge of blasphemy against those supernatural beings. (2 PETER 2:9–11 NLT)

Interpretations vary. Generally it's held that Peter refers to false teachers who either disputed the existence of angels/demons or boasted they could control such spirits. Perhaps the "supernatural beings" are a kind of fallen angels whose powers are inferior (after their fall) to those of God's angels; when the latter report to him on the former's actions, they state the facts without exaggeration or bitterness. Some believe these "beings" are God's angels; though the false teachers slander them, they don't speak against those teachers. Another idea relates to the Jewish belief that spiritual beings ruled nations and guided their leaders; maybe the false teachers spoke against earthly authorities and, thus, angelic authorities behind them.

─────── **THE FATE OF ANGELS WHO SINNED** ───────

The angels who did not keep their positions of authority but abandoned their proper dwelling—these [the Lord] has kept in darkness, bound with everlasting chains for judgment on the great Day. (JUDE 1:6 NIV)

> *These angels may have rebelled either when Satan fell or in some other sin (see comments on 2 Peter 2:4). Some say "positions of authority" were the angels' roles as spiritual authorities over the world's nations (i.e., they left their assignments, came to earth, became the devil and his demons).*

─────── **THOSE WHO SLANDER ANGELS** ───────

On the strength of their dreams these ungodly people pollute their own bodies, reject authority and heap abuse on celestial beings. But even the archangel Michael, when he was disputing with the devil about the body of Moses, did not himself dare to condemn him for slander but said, "The Lord rebuke you!" (JUDE 1:8-9 NIV; *see comments for* 2 PETER 2:9-11).

─────── **CHRIST'S RETURN WITH HIS HOLY ONES** ───────

Enoch, who lived in the seventh generation after Adam, prophesied about these people. He said, "Listen! The Lord is coming with countless thousands of his holy ones to execute judgment on the people of the world. He will convict every person of all the ungodly things they have done and for all the insults that ungodly sinners have spoken against him" (JUDE 1:14-15 NLT).

> *Some believe "holy ones" here refers to God's angels. Others contend it refers to raptured saints returning to earth with the Lord.*

121

7
Angels and Demons
in Revelation

The Bible's final book is addressed to seven first-century churches. Some say its events refer primarily to happenings at that time. Some say they encompass the span of church history or pertain to the future. Some believe it isn't historical or prophetic but meant to teach on the struggle between good and evil. Our focus is on what it says about angels and demons in various forms.

THE UNVEILING

This is the revelation of Jesus Christ. God gave it to him to show his servants the things that must happen soon. He sent this revelation through his angel to his servant John. John testified about what he saw: God's word and the testimony about Jesus Christ. (REVELATION 1:1–2 GOD'S WORD)

"His angel" is intermediary; signs and visions come to John as he guides.

───── **THE MEANING OF THE STARS AND LAMPSTANDS** ─────

The mystery of the seven stars that you saw in my right hand and of the seven golden lampstands is this: The seven stars are the angels of the seven churches, and the seven lampstands are the seven churches. **(REVELATION 1:20 NIV)**

> *"Angels" here may refer to God-sent human messengers (pastors or key elders) who represent them. They could be heavenly angels (a guardian for each congregation) or personify each church's prevailing spirit. Jesus dictates messages for John to give each "angel" (Revelation 2–3); as these messengers likely were human, we won't address most such passages here.*

───────── **THE MESSAGE TO SMYRNA** ─────────

I know how you are suffering, how poor you are—but you are rich. I also know that those who claim to be Jews slander you. They are the synagogue of Satan. Don't be afraid of what you are going to suffer. The devil is going to throw some of you into prison so that you may be tested. Your suffering will go on for ten days. Be faithful until death, and I will give you the crown of life. **(REVELATION 2:9–10 GOD'S WORD)**

> *The synagogue wasn't overtly devoted to Satan; Jesus associates him with those who were slandering believers. Satan used prejudices to persecute Christians, who generally were charged with violating emperor-worship laws only if an informer went to Roman authorities. "Jews in Smyrna were reportedly fulfilling this function" by then,*

and synagogue exclusions could have led to more direct persecution by the Romans (Craig S. Keener).

THE MESSAGE TO PERGAMUM

I see where you live, right under the shadow of Satan's throne. But you continue boldly in my Name; you never once denied my Name, even when the pressure was worst, when they martyred Antipas, my witness who stayed faithful to me on Satan's turf. **(REVELATION 2:13 THE MESSAGE)**

"Satan's throne" (not the seat from which he ruled) probably refers to the official center of emperor worship in what then was known as Asia.

THE MESSAGE TO THYATIRA

The rest of you in Thyatira . . . don't hold on to Jezebel's teaching . . . [and] haven't learned what are called the deep things of Satan. **(REVELATION 2:24 GOD'S WORD)**

"Deep things" were promised "spiritual secrets" through false religions.

THE MESSAGE TO SARDIS

All who are victorious will be clothed in white. I will never erase their names from the Book of Life, but I will announce before my Father and his angels that they are mine. **(REVELATION 3:5 NLT)**

Given the angels' role in separating believers from unbelievers at the end, it's important that they know who belongs to Jesus.

THE MESSAGE TO PHILADELPHIA

I will force those who belong to Satan's synagogue—those liars who say they are Jews but are not—to come and bow down at your feet. They will acknowledge that you are the ones I love. (REVELATION 3:9 NLT)

Jesus again metaphorically refers to hostile Jews (cf. Revelation 2:9).

THE THRONE IN HEAVEN

Before the throne there was something that looked like a sea of glass, clear like crystal.

In the center and around the throne were four living creatures with eyes all over them, in front and in back. The first living creature was like a lion. The second was like a calf. The third had a face like a man. The fourth was like a flying eagle. Each . . . had six wings and was covered all over with eyes, inside and out. Day and night they never stop saying:

"Holy, holy, holy is the Lord God Almighty.

He was, he is, and he is coming."

These living creatures give glory, honor, and thanks to the One who sits on the throne, who lives forever and ever. Then the twenty-four elders bow down before the One who sits on the throne, and they worship him who lives forever and ever. They put their crowns down before the throne and say:

"You are worthy, our Lord and God,

to receive glory and honor and power,

because you made all things.

Everything existed and was made,

because you wanted it" (REVELATION 4:6–11 NCV).

The "living creatures"—by God's throne, leading his worship—may be an exalted angelic order similar to the cherubim mentioned by Isaiah and Ezekiel. (They exhibit features associated with both cherubim and seraphim.) The many eyes are thought to symbolize vast knowledge.

THE LAMB TAKES THE SCROLL

I saw a strong angel proclaiming with a loud voice, "Who is worthy to open the scroll and to loose its seals?" (REVELATION 5:2 NKJV).

"Strong" may pertain to the angel's voice or high rank. The next verse says no one in heaven or on earth could open the scroll, indicating his voice being heard by all of creation.

EXALTING THE LAMB

I looked and heard the voice of many angels, numbering thousands upon thousands, and ten thousand times ten thousand. They encircled the throne and the living creatures and the elders. In a loud voice they were saying:
   "Worthy is the Lamb, who was slain,
   to receive power and wealth and wisdom and strength
   and honor and glory and praise!" (REVELATION 5:11–12 NIV).

Angels, too many to count, sing praises before God's throne.

THE FOUR LIVING CREATURES

I watched while the Lamb opened the first of the seven seals. I heard one of the four living creatures say with a voice like thunder, "Come!" I looked, and there before me was a white horse.

The rider on the horse held a bow, and he was given a crown, and he rode out, determined to win the victory.

When the Lamb opened the second seal, I heard the second living creature say, "Come!" Then another horse came out, a red one. Its rider was given power to take away peace from the earth and to make people kill each other, and he was given a big sword.

When the Lamb opened the third seal, I heard the third living creature say, "Come!" I looked, and there before me was a black horse, and its rider held a pair of scales in his hand. Then I heard something that sounded like a voice coming from the middle of the four living creatures. The voice said, "A quart of wheat for a day's pay, and three quarts of barley for a day's pay, and do not damage the olive oil and wine!"

When the Lamb opened the fourth seal, I heard the voice of the fourth living creature say, "Come!" I looked, and there before me was a pale horse. Its rider was named death, and Hades was following close behind him. They were given power over a fourth of the earth to kill people by war, by starvation, by disease, and by the wild animals of the earth. (REVELATION 6:1–8 NCV; *also see comments on* REVELATION 4:6–11)

--- THE SERVANTS OF GOD ---

I saw four angels standing at the four corners of the earth. They were holding back the four winds of the earth to keep them from blowing on the land, the sea, or any tree. I saw another angel coming from the east with the seal of the living God. He cried out in a loud voice to the four angels who had been allowed to harm the land and sea, "Don't harm the land, the sea, or the trees until we have put the seal on the foreheads of the servants of our God" (REVELATION 7:1–3 GOD'S WORD).

The four angels have power to carry out God's judgment, and his seal signifies ownership and protection. The other angel may be either a messenger of God or Christ himself; he has authority to command the other angels; his speech in the plural leads some to say he's speaking for God.

—————— SURROUNDING GOD'S THRONE ——————

All the angels were standing around the throne and around the elders and the four living beings. And they fell before the throne with their faces to the ground and worshiped God. (**REVELATION 7:11 NLT**)

Even God's holy angels and the living creatures, accustomed to his presence, fall to their faces before him in utter submission and adoration.

—————— SEVEN ANGELS WITH TRUMPETS ——————

I saw the seven angels who stand before God, and seven trumpets were given to them.

Another angel came and stood at the altar, holding a golden censer; and much incense was given to him, so that he might add it to the prayers of all the saints on the golden altar which was before the throne. And the smoke of the incense, with the prayers of the saints, went up before God out of the angel's hand. Then the angel took the censer and filled it with the fire of the altar, and threw it to the earth; and there followed peals of thunder and sounds and flashes of lightning and an earthquake.

And the seven angels who had the seven trumpets prepared themselves to sound them.

The first sounded, and there came hail and fire, mixed with blood, and they were thrown to the earth; and a third of the earth was burned up, and a third of the trees were burned up, and all the green grass was burned up.

The second angel sounded, and something like a great mountain burning with fire was thrown into the sea; and a third of the sea became blood, and a third of the creatures which were in the sea and had life, died; and a third of the ships were destroyed.

The third angel sounded, and a great star fell from heaven, burning like a torch, and it fell on a third of the rivers and on the springs of waters. The name of the star is called Wormwood; and a third of the waters became wormwood, and many men died from the [bitter] waters. . . .

The fourth angel sounded, and a third of the sun and a third of the moon and a third of the stars were struck, so that a third of them would be darkened and the day would not shine for a third of it, and the night in the same way.

Then I looked, and I heard an eagle flying in midheaven, saying with a loud voice, "Woe, woe, woe to those who dwell on the earth, because of the remaining blasts of the trumpet of the three angels who are about to sound!" **(REVELATION 8:2–13 NASB)**.

"Another angel" presents the church's prayers to God but doesn't act as a mediator to make them acceptable to him. Seven trumpets signal limited judgments to warn of the coming destruction and call people to repent.

THE FIFTH TRUMPET SOUNDS

The fifth angel sounded his trumpet, and I saw a star that had fallen from the sky to the earth. The star was given the key to the shaft of the Abyss. When he opened the Abyss, smoke rose from it like the smoke from a gigantic furnace. The sun and sky were darkened by the smoke from the Abyss. And out of the smoke locusts came down on the earth and were given power like that of scorpions of the earth. They were told not to harm the grass of the earth or any plant or tree, but only those people who did not have the seal of God on their foreheads. They were not allowed to kill them, but only to torture them for five months. And the agony they suffered was like that of the sting of a scorpion when it strikes. During those days people will seek death, but will not find it; they will long to die, but death will elude them.

The locusts looked like horses prepared for battle. On their heads they wore something like crowns of gold, and their faces resembled human faces. Their hair was like women's hair, and their teeth were like lions' teeth. They had breastplates like breastplates of iron, and the sound of their wings was like the thundering of many horses and chariots rushing into battle. They had tails with stingers like scorpions, and . . . power to torment people for five months. They had as king over them the angel of the Abyss, whose name in Hebrew is Abaddon, and in Greek is Apollyon. (REVELATION 9:1–11 NIV)

This "angel of the Abyss" ("destroyer") likely is demonic, perhaps a chief leader or Satan himself. The "locusts" are demons, not insects.

——————— THE SIXTH TRUMPET SOUNDS ———————

Then the sixth angel sounded: And I heard a voice from the four horns of the golden altar which is before God, saying to the sixth angel who had the trumpet, "Release the four angels who are bound at the great river Euphrates." So the four angels, who had been prepared for the hour and day and month and year, were released to kill a third of mankind. (REVELATION 9:13–15 NKJV)

Not to be confused with the earlier "four" (see Revelation 7), these are fallen angels God had bound but now releases to carry out his judgment.

131

—————— SURVIVORS ARE UNREPENTANT ——————

The people who survived these plagues still did not turn to me and change the way they were thinking and acting. If they had, they would have stopped worshiping demons and idols made of gold, silver, bronze, stone, and wood, which cannot see, hear, or walk. (REVELATION 9:20 GOD'S WORD)

People still alive on earth persist in worshiping demons and human objects.

—————— THE ANGEL AND THE SMALL SCROLL ——————

I saw another powerful angel coming down from heaven dressed in a cloud with a rainbow over his head. His face was like the sun, and his legs were like pillars of fire. The angel was holding a small scroll open in his hand. He put his right foot on the sea and his left foot on the land. Then he shouted loudly like the roaring of a lion. And when he shouted, the voices of seven thunders spoke. When the seven thunders spoke, I started to write. But I heard a voice from heaven say, "Keep hidden what the seven thunders said, and do not write them down."

Then the angel I saw standing on the sea and on the land raised his right hand to heaven, and he made a promise by the power of the One who lives forever and ever. He is the One who made the skies and all that is in them, the earth and all that is in it, and the sea and all that is in it. The angel promised, "There will be no more waiting! In the days when the seventh angel is ready to blow his trumpet, God's secret will be finished. This secret is the Good News God told to his servants, the prophets."

Then I heard the same voice from heaven again, saying to me: "Go and take the open scroll that is in the hand of the angel that is standing on the sea and on the land."

So I went to the angel and told him to give me the small scroll. And he said to me, "Take the scroll and eat it. It will be sour in your stomach, but in your mouth it will be sweet as honey." So I took the small scroll from the angel's hand and ate it. In my mouth it tasted sweet as honey, but after I ate it, it was sour in my stomach. **(REVELATION 10:1–10 NCV)**

Some believe "another powerful angel" is more than an angel; his attributes may suggest a divine figure, i.e., Christ. Some also say "right foot on the sea, left on the land" shows Jesus demonstrating authority over the earth. (Others say this possibly is Michael.) The word translated "another" means "one of the same kind," notes John MacArthur; Christ isn't akin to the created angel previously mentioned. As Christ commissioned an angel to deliver God's revelation to John, intermediately, some say it's unlikely Christ then would be interacting with John amid that revelation.

THE BEAST SLAYS GOD'S WITNESSES

When the witnesses finish their testimony, the beast which comes from the bottomless pit will fight them, conquer them, and kill them. **(REVELATION 11:7 GOD'S WORD)**

"Beast" may be Satan in human form, a counterfeit Christ (antichrist); rising from the pit attests to his demonic nature. This first of thirty-six "beast" references includes little explanation; some say John assumed readers already would be familiar with certain descriptions (e.g., Daniel 7:3, 11). "Beast of the Abyss" was a common reference to the antichrist.

THE SEVENTH TRUMPET SOUNDS

The seventh angel sounded his trumpet and . . . loud voices in heaven . . . said:

"The kingdom of the world has become the kingdom of our Lord and of his Messiah, and he will reign for ever and ever" (**REVELATION 11:15 NIV;** *also see comments on* **REVELATION 8:2–13**).

──────────── **THE WOMAN AND THE DRAGON** ────────────

I saw [in heaven] a large red dragon with seven heads and ten horns, with seven crowns on his heads. His tail swept away one-third of the stars in the sky, and he threw them to the earth. He stood in front of the woman as she was about to give birth, ready to devour her baby as soon as it was born. . . . Then there was war in heaven. Michael and his angels fought against the dragon and his angels. And the dragon lost the battle, and he and his angels were forced out of heaven. This great dragon— the ancient serpent called the devil, or Satan, the one deceiving the whole world—was thrown down to the earth with all his angels. (**REVELATION 12:3–4, 7–9 NLT**)

The dragon's description symbolizes Satan's murderous, evil character. Many think sweeping to earth a third of the stars refers to Satan taking a third of the angels at his original fall and these spirits becoming his demons. The woman likely represents Israel, who gave birth to the Messiah; Satan unsuccessfully tried to destroy the baby through Herod. Many say the war between Michael's angels and the dragon's forces occurs in the future great tribulation.

──────────── **THE ACCUSER SHALL BE CAST DOWN** ────────────

I heard a loud voice saying in heaven, "Now salvation, and strength, and the kingdom of our God, and the power of His Christ have come, for the accuser of our brethren, who accused them before our God day and night, has been cast down. And they overcame him by the blood of the Lamb and by the word of their testimony, and they did not love their lives to the death. Therefore rejoice, O heavens, and you who dwell in them! Woe to the inhabitants of the earth and the sea! For the devil has come down to you, having great wrath, because he knows that he has a short time" (**REVELATION 12:10–12 NKJV**).

Many believe this evokes not the original demonic fall but final exclusion from heaven after battling Michael's angels. Satan's accusations are of no effect; the Lamb's blood (from Christ's sacrifice) covers his people's sins. Facing his impending demise, Satan will take out his rage upon the earth.

──── **SATAN'S ASSAULT ON ISRAEL AND THE CHURCH** ────

The dragon . . . pursued the woman who had given birth to the male child. The woman was given the two wings of a great eagle, so that she might fly to the place prepared for her in the wilderness, where she would be taken care of for a time, times and half a time, out of the serpent's reach. Then from his mouth the serpent spewed water like a river, to overtake the woman and sweep her away with the torrent. But the earth helped the woman by opening its mouth and swallowing the river that the dragon had spewed out of his mouth. Then the dragon was enraged at the woman and went off to make war against the rest of her offspring—those who keep God's commands and hold fast their testimony about Jesus. (**REVELATION 12:13–17 NIV**)

Satan will direct intense fury; Israel will be protected three and a half years. Some believe the torrent may represent invasion by a great army, others suggest the flood refers to Satan trying to destroy God's people through false teaching. Satan then will rage against believers in general.

THE BEAST OF THE SEA

The dragon stood on the sand of the seashore.

Then I saw a beast coming up out of the sea, having ten horns and seven heads, and on his horns were ten diadems, and on his heads were blasphemous names. . . . [He] was like a leopard, and his feet were like those of a bear, and his mouth like the mouth of a lion. And the dragon gave him his power and his throne and great authority. I saw one of his heads as if it had been slain, and his fatal wound was healed. And the whole earth was amazed and followed after the beast; they worshiped the dragon because he gave his authority to the beast; and they worshiped the beast, saying, "Who is like the beast, and who is able to wage war with him?" There was given to him a mouth speaking arrogant words and blasphemies, and authority to act for forty-two months. . . . And he opened his mouth in blasphemies against God, to blaspheme His name and His tabernacle, that is, those who dwell in heaven.

It was also given to him to make war with the saints and to overcome them, and authority over every tribe and people and tongue and nation was given to him. All who dwell on the earth will worship him, everyone whose name has not been written from the foundation of the world in the book of life of the Lamb who has been slain. If anyone has an ear, let him hear. If anyone is destined for captivity, to captivity he goes; if anyone kills with the sword, with the sword he must be killed. Here is the perseverance and the faith of the saints. (**REVELATION 13:1–10 NASB**)

Rising from the sea may mean being a Gentile or rising from the haunt of demons. The seven heads may refer to successive world empires or to Rome (founded on seven hills; many emperors considered themselves gods). The ten horns may symbolize kings, or all the

*world's political/military powers. Satan confers power and author-
ity; the beast may be a demon-possessed man or Satan in human
form. The head slain-then-healed may represent a destroyed/revived
kingdom, or the beast (antichrist?) might fake death to amaze with
his "miraculous" resurrection. The world now worships Satan and
the beast; the world's leader brings war against the saints.*

THE BEAST OF THE EARTH

I saw another beast coming up out of the earth, and he had two
horns like a lamb and spoke like a dragon. And he exercises
all the authority of the first beast in his presence, and causes
the earth and those who dwell in it to worship the first beast,
whose deadly wound was healed. He performs great signs, so
that he even makes fire come down from heaven on the earth in
the sight of men. And he deceives those who dwell on the earth
by those signs which he was granted to do in the sight of the
beast, telling those who dwell on the earth to make an image
to the beast who was wounded by the sword and lived. He was
granted power to give breath to the image of the beast, that
the image of the beast should both speak and cause as many
as would not worship the image of the beast to be killed. He
causes all, both small and great, rich and poor, free and slave,
to receive a mark on their right hand or on their foreheads, and
that no one may buy or sell except one who has the mark or the
name of the beast, or the number of his name.

Here is wisdom. Let him who has understanding calculate
the number of the beast . . . the number of a man: . . . 666.
(REVELATION 13:11–18 NKJV)

*This false prophet appears gentle and peaceful but is full of deceit.
Dragon, beast, and false prophet form a counterfeit trinity (Satan
falsely likened to the Father, the beast to the Son, the false prophet*

to the Spirit). The false prophet shares satanic authority, possessing or imitating supernatural power, making fire appear in the sky and an idol to speak. He requires everyone to wear the beast's "mark" to buy or sell.

THE THREE ANGELS

I saw another angel flying overhead with the everlasting Good News to spread to [all of] those who live on earth. . . . The angel said in a loud voice, "Fear God and give him glory, because the time has come for him to judge. Worship the one who made heaven and earth, the sea and springs."

Another angel, a second one, followed him, and said, "Fallen! Babylon the Great has fallen! She has made all the nations drink the wine of her passionate sexual sins."

Another angel, a third one, followed them, and said in a loud voice, "Whoever worships the beast or its statue, whoever is branded on his forehead or his hand, will drink the wine of God's fury, which has been poured unmixed into the cup of God's anger. Then he will be tortured by fiery sulfur in the presence of the holy angels and the lamb. The smoke from their torture will go up forever and ever. There will be no rest day or night for those who worship the beast or its statue, or for anyone branded with its name" (REVELATION 14:6–11 GOD'S WORD).

An angel proclaims to the world the gospel—God forgives sin and invites all who repent and believe into his kingdom—and urges all to turn to him because judgment nears. Some think the second announcement refers to Rome's fall; others think it means the political and religious system of the beast (antichrist). A third angel warns of the judgment (which the holy angels witness) awaiting those who worship the beast and accept his mark.

——————— THE HARVEST OF THE EARTH ———————

Another angel came out of the temple and called in a loud voice to him who was sitting on the cloud, "Take your sickle and reap, because the time to reap has come, for the harvest of the earth is ripe." So he who was seated on the cloud swung his sickle over the earth, and the earth was harvested.

Another angel came out of the temple in heaven [with] . . . a sharp sickle. Still another angel, who had charge of the fire, came from the altar and called in a loud voice to him who had the sharp sickle, "Take your sharp sickle and gather the clusters of grapes from the earth's vine, because its grapes are ripe." The angel swung his sickle on the earth, gathered its grapes and threw them into the great winepress of God's wrath. **(REVELATION 14:15–19 NIV)**

> *That an angel commands the one on the cloud ("like a son of man," v. 14) leads some to say the one isn't Christ, who wouldn't be receiving directions from an angel. Some think this harvest means gathering saints for Christ's return; others think they're unbelievers being gathered for judgment.*

——————— SEVEN ANGELS, SEVEN PLAGUES ———————

I saw another sign in heaven, great and marvelous: seven angels having the seven last plagues, for in them the wrath of God is complete.

And I saw something like a sea of glass mingled with fire, and those who have the victory over the beast, over his image and over his mark and over the number of his name, standing on the sea of glass, having harps of God. . . . After these things I looked, and behold, the temple of the tabernacle of the testimony in heaven was opened. And out of the temple came the seven angels having the seven plagues, clothed in pure bright linen, and having their chests girded with golden bands. Then one of the four living creatures gave to the seven angels seven golden bowls full of the wrath of God who lives forever and ever. The temple was filled with smoke from the glory of God and from His power, and no one was able to enter the temple till the seven plagues of the seven angels were completed. (**REVELATION 15:1–2, 5–8 NKJV**)

The overcomers, now in heaven, likely are martyrs. A living creature gives the bowls of wrath to the seven angels, whose linen garments represent holiness and purity. Their golden bands depict riches and royalty.

―――― **THE SEVEN ANGELS POUR OUT THEIR BOWLS** ――――

I heard a loud voice from the temple saying to the seven angels, "Go, pour out the seven bowls of God's wrath on the earth."

The first angel went and poured out his bowl on the land, and ugly, festering sores broke out on the people who had the mark of the beast and worshiped its image.

The second angel poured out his bowl on the sea, and it turned into blood like that of a dead person, and every living thing in the sea died.

The third angel poured out his bowl on the rivers and springs of water, and they became blood. Then I heard the angel in charge of the waters say:

"You are just in these judgments, O Holy One,

you who are and who were;

for they have shed the blood of your holy people and your prophets,

and you have given them blood to drink as they deserve."

And I heard the altar respond:

"Yes, Lord God Almighty,
true and just are your judgments."

The fourth angel poured out his bowl on the sun, and the sun was allowed to scorch people with fire. They were seared by the intense heat and they cursed the name of God, who had control over these plagues, but they refused to repent and glorify him.

The fifth angel poured out his bowl on the throne of the beast, and its kingdom was plunged into darkness. People gnawed their tongues in agony and cursed the God of heaven because of their pains and their sores, but they refused to repent of what they had done.

The sixth angel poured out his bowl on the great river Euphrates, and its water was dried up to prepare the way for the kings from the East. Then I saw three impure spirits that looked like frogs; they came out of the mouth of the dragon, out of the mouth of the beast and out of the mouth of the false prophet. They are demonic spirits that perform signs, and they go out to the kings of the whole world, to gather them for the battle on the great day of God Almighty.

"Look, I come like a thief! Blessed is the one who stays awake and remains clothed, so as not to go naked and be shamefully exposed."

Then they gathered the kings together to the place that in Hebrew is called Armageddon.

The seventh angel poured out his bowl into the air, and out of the temple came a loud voice from the throne, saying, "It is done!" (REVELATION 16:1–17 NIV).

The beast-worshipers are punished with open sores. The angel praises God's justice. Wrath on the beast's throne (actual throne or capital city) is an assault on evil's power source. The frog-like demons may represent deceptive speech to persuade leaders to join the battle against God.

One of the Seven Angels Speaks
of Babylon and the Beast

"Come here, I will show you the judgment of the great harlot who sits on many waters, with whom the kings of the earth committed acts of immorality, and those who dwell on the earth were made drunk with the wine of her immorality." And he carried me away in the Spirit into a wilderness; and I saw a woman sitting on a scarlet beast, full of blasphemous names, having seven heads and ten horns. The woman was clothed in purple and scarlet, and adorned with gold and precious stones and pearls, having in her hand a gold cup full of abominations and of the unclean things of her immorality, and on her forehead a name was written, a mystery, "BABYLON THE GREAT, THE MOTHER OF HARLOTS AND OF THE ABOMINATIONS OF THE EARTH." And I saw the woman drunk with the blood of the saints, and with the blood of the witnesses of Jesus. When I saw her, I wondered greatly.

And the angel said to me, "Why do you wonder? I will tell you the mystery of the woman and of the beast that carries her, which has the seven heads and the ten horns.

"The beast that you saw was, and is not, and is about to come up out of the abyss and go to destruction. And those who dwell on the earth, whose name has not been written in the book of life from the foundation of the world, will wonder when they see the beast, that he was and is not and will come. Here is the mind which has wisdom. The seven heads are seven mountains on which the woman sits, and they are seven kings; five have fallen, one is, the other has not yet come; and when he comes, he must remain a little while. The beast which was and is not, is himself also an eighth and is one of the seven, and he goes to destruction. The ten horns which you saw are ten kings who have not yet received a kingdom, but they receive authority as kings with the beast for one hour. These have one purpose, and they give their power and authority to the beast.

"These will wage war against the Lamb, and the Lamb will overcome them, because He is Lord of lords and King of kings, and those who are with Him are the called and chosen and faithful."

And he said to me, "The waters which you saw where the harlot sits, are peoples and multitudes and nations and tongues.

"And the ten horns which you saw, and the beast, these will hate the harlot and will make her desolate and naked, and will eat her flesh and will burn her up with fire. For God has put it in their hearts to execute His purpose by having a common purpose, and by giving their kingdom to the beast, until the words of God will be fulfilled" (REVELATION 17:1–17 NASB).

Beast (antichrist) carrying harlot (Babylon) may suggest the world's satanic leader supporting/operating under a false religious system. This is mutually beneficial, wherein the state's coercion promulgates the false faith and the beast uses the system for his purposes ("unity," world power). After a time, he'll destroy this system and command all worship to himself.

THE FALL OF BABYLON

I saw another angel coming down from heaven, having great authority, and the earth was illuminated with his glory. And he cried mightily with a loud voice, saying, "Babylon the great is fallen . . . and has become a dwelling place of demons, a prison for every foul spirit, and a cage for every unclean and hated bird! For all the nations have drunk of the wine of the wrath of her fornication, the kings of the earth have committed fornication with her, and the merchants . . . have become rich through the abundance of her luxury." . . .

Then a mighty angel took up . . . [a great millstone] and threw it into the sea, saying, "Thus with violence the great city Babylon shall be thrown down, and shall not be found anymore. The sound of harpists, musicians, flutists, and trumpeters shall not be heard in you anymore. No craftsman of any craft shall be found in you anymore, and the sound of a millstone shall not be heard in you anymore. The light of a lamp shall not shine in you anymore, and the voice of bridegroom and bride shall not be heard in you anymore. For your merchants were the great men of the earth, for by your sorcery all the nations were deceived. And in her was found the blood of prophets and saints, and of all who were slain on the earth" (**REVELATION 18:1–3, 21–24 NKJV**).

Angelic light would be immeasurably glorious if the beast's kingdom already has plunged into darkness (see Revelation 16:10). "Babylon" falling shows man's achievements now to be nothing but demonic haunts.

THE MARRIAGE OF THE LAMB

"Write this: Blessed are those who have been invited to the wedding meal of the Lamb!" And the angel said, "These are the true words of God."

Then I bowed down at the angel's feet to worship him, but he said to me, "Do not worship me! I am a servant like you and your brothers and sisters who have the message of Jesus. Worship God, because the message about Jesus is the spirit that gives all prophecy" (**REVELATION 19:9–10 NCV**).

Angels and people are both servants of the one God.

——————— The Great Banquet of God ———————

I saw an angel standing in the sun, shouting to the vultures flying high in the sky: "Come! Gather together for the great banquet God has prepared. Come and eat the flesh of kings, generals, and strong warriors; of horses and their riders; and of all humanity, both free and slave, small and great" (REVELATION 19:17–18 NLT).

Angels shining with God's glory can be seen even in front of the sun.

——————— Doom of the Beast and False Prophet ———————

I saw the beast and the kings of the earth and their armies assembled to make war against Him who sat on the horse and against His army.

The beast was seized, and with him the false prophet who performed the signs in his presence, by which he deceived those who had received the mark of the beast and those who worshiped his image; these two were thrown alive into the lake of fire which burns with brimstone. (REVELATION 19:19–20 NASB)

> *Opposing God to the end, the beast (likely Satan in human form) readies to war against Jesus (see v. 11). Missing "details" may indicate a short, one-sided conflict—an act of judgment. The false prophet has deceived all who followed the beast; they and all they represent will be utterly destroyed.*

——————— An Angel Overpowers the Devil ———————

I saw an angel coming down from heaven, holding the key to the bottomless pit and a large chain in his hand. He overpowered the serpent, that ancient snake, named Devil and Satan. The angel chained up the serpent for 1,000 years. He threw it into the bottomless pit. The angel shut and sealed the pit over the serpent to keep it from deceiving the nations anymore until the 1,000 years were over. After that it must be set free for a little while. (REVELATION 20:1–3 GOD'S WORD)

When God is ready to remove Satan and his influence, he needs only one angel with a chain and a key. That said, the means described for restraining Satan may symbolize restriction on satanic power for a long time. Many believe this refers to a future golden age of peace. (Some say "1,000 years" represents the gospel's spread in this current age.) Some believe God then will use Satan to "clean house," as some who live during this period still will rebel against God.

THE THOUSAND YEARS

I saw thrones, and the people sitting on them had been given the authority to judge. And I saw the souls of those who had been beheaded for their testimony about Jesus and for proclaiming the word of God. They had not worshiped the beast or his statue, nor accepted his mark on their forehead or their hands. They all came to life again, and they reigned with Christ for a thousand years. (REVELATION 20:4 NLT)

God will resurrect and reward the martyrs who died for their faith.

THE DEFEAT OF SATAN

When the thousand years are over, Satan will be set free from his prison. Then he will go out to trick the nations in all the earth—Gog and Magog—to gather them for battle. There are so many people they will be like sand on the seashore. And Satan's army marched across the earth and gathered around the camp of God's people and the city God loves. But fire came down from heaven and burned them up. And Satan, who tricked them, was thrown into the lake of burning sulfur with the beast and the false prophet. There they will be punished day and night forever and ever. (REVELATION 20:7–10 NCV)

Satan again deceives; God intervenes and inflicts everlasting punishment.

THE NEW JERUSALEM

One of the seven angels who had the seven bowls full of the seven last plagues came and said to me, "Come, I will show you the bride, the wife of the Lamb." And he carried me away in the Spirit to a mountain great and high, and showed me the Holy City, Jerusalem, coming down out of heaven from God. . . . It had a great, high wall with twelve gates, and with twelve angels at the gates. On the gates were written the names of the twelve tribes of Israel. . . . The angel who talked with me had a measuring rod of gold to measure the city, its gates and its walls. The city was laid out like a square, as long as it was wide. He measured the city with the rod and found it to be 12,000 stadia in length, and as wide and high as it is long. The angel measured its wall using human measurement, and it was 144 cubits thick. (REVELATION 21:9–10, 12, 15–17 NIV)

Angels will securely guard the gates of God's city.

THE RIVER OF LIFE

The angel showed me a river with the water of life, clear as crystal, flowing from the throne of God and of the Lamb. (REVELATION 22:1 NLT)

The angel reveals imagery to complete the story of God and his people. The living water of which Jesus spoke flows from God's throne.

GOD'S WORDS DON'T FAIL

These words are trustworthy and true. The Lord, the God who inspires the prophets, sent his angel to show his servants the things that must soon take place. (REVELATION 22:6 NIV)

The angel reconfirms that he's spoken for God and verifies the revelation.

"WORSHIP GOD"

I, John, am the one who heard and saw these things. And when I heard and saw, I fell down to worship at the feet of the angel who showed me these things. But he said to me, "Do not do that. I am a fellow servant of yours and of your brethren the prophets and of those who heed the words of this book. Worship God" (REVELATION 22:8–9 NASB; *also see* REVELATION 19:9–10).

JESUS ATTESTS TO THE MESSAGE'S VALIDITY

I, Jesus, sent my Angel to testify to these things for the churches. I'm the Root and Branch of David, the Bright Morning Star. (REVELATION 22:16 THE MESSAGE)

Jesus reconfirms authorizing the angel to deliver the revelation.

Index of Frequently Asked Questions About Angels and Demons

Angels and their evil counterparts, the fallen angels who became Satan and his demons, inspire both fascination and fear. *Everything the Bible Says About Angels and Demons* makes it quick and easy to learn more about them. Here is a sampling of just some of the common questions people have about angels and demons and where the answers can be found in this book.

What is an angel? Exodus 23:20–23; Psalm 103:20–21; Hebrews 1:13–14

Who is Satan? Isaiah 14:12–14; Ephesians 2:2; 1 Peter 5:8–9; Jude 1:6; Revelation 12:3–4, 7–9; 20:1–3

What do angels look like? Genesis 19; Isaiah 6:1–7; Judges 6:11–24; 13:2–23; Ezekiel 1:4–28; 10:1–22; Luke 24:1–8; Hebrews 13:2; Revelation 15:5–8

Who is the angel of the Lord? Genesis 16:7–13; Judges 2:1–5; 6:11–24; 13:2–23

What does the Bible say about guardian angels? Psalm 34:7; 91:9–12; Matthew 18:10; Acts 12:13–16

Do people become angels when they die? Psalm 8:4–5; Hebrews 2:14–16

References Consulted

Angels Among Us. Ron Rhodes (Harvest House, 1994).

Angels: God's Secret Agents. Billy Graham (Word, 1994).

The Bible Exposition Commentary, Vols. 1–2. Warren Wiersbe (Victor, 1989).

ESV Study Bible (Crossway Bibles, 2008).

Evangelical Commentary on the Bible. Walter A. Elwell, ed. (Baker, 1989).

Hard Sayings of the Bible. Walter C. Kaiser Jr., et al. (InterVarsity, 1996).

The Illustrated Bible Dictionary (Tyndale, 1980).

The IVP Bible Background Commentary: New Testament. Craig S. Keener (InterVarsity, 1993).

The KJV Parallel Bible Commentary. Jerry Falwell, exec. ed. (Nelson, 1994).

The MacArthur Bible Commentary. John MacArthur (Nelson, 2005).

The NIV Study Bible (Zondervan, 1985).

Topical Analysis of the Bible: With the New International Version. Walter A. Elwell, gen. ed., et al. (Baker, 1991).

---------------------------- ONLINE ----------------------------

Barnes' Notes on the Bible

Biblegateway.com

Clarke's Commentary on the Bible

David Guzik's Commentaries
Geneva Study Bible
Gill's Exposition of the Entire Bible
Jamieson-Fausset-Brown Commentary
Keil and Delitzsch OT Commentary
Matthew Henry's Concise Commentary
Matthew Henry's Whole Bible Commentary
Wesley's Notes on the Bible

More Insight
from God's Word

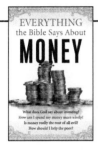

How people deal with money matters to God. In fact, it is one of the most frequently mentioned subjects in the Bible. In this short, handy book, all the scriptural references to money have been collected and explained in a clear and concise format. Hear what God has to say about everything related to money, including working, saving, tithing—and more!

Everything the Bible Says About Money

Have you ever wanted to ask God what heaven is like? It turns out, He's already told us! The Bible is filled with passages that explain what heaven looks like, what we'll do there, and how to get there in the first place—and this book has carefully collected and organized them all! Here you will find all the scriptural reference to heaven, as well as brief, clear explanations and insights from trustworthy commentaries.

Everything the Bible Says About Heaven

BETHANYHOUSE